THE DVD BOOK OF
TOTTENHAM HOTSPUR

Written by Graham Betts

THE DVD BOOK OF
TOTTENHAM HOTSPUR

This edition first published in the UK in 2007
By Green Umbrella Publishing

© Green Umbrella Publishing 2008

www.gupublishing.co.uk

Publishers Jules Gammond & Vanessa Gardner

Printed and bound in China

ISBN: 978-1-906229-92-4

Contents

Allen Family

ONE OF THE GREAT FOOTBALLING families, they have provided Spurs with three key players over the last five decades. Les Allen was born in Dagenham on 4th September 1937 and joined Spurs from Chelsea in December 1959 as part of a deal that saw Johnny Brooks make the opposite journey. Les linked especially well up front with Bobby Smith and scored five of Spurs' goals in the 13-2 cup replay win over Crewe Alexandra in 1960. It was the following season, however, that both Les and Spurs hit top gear, winning the League and Cup double, with Les an ever present and netting 27 goals. The arrival of Jimmy Greaves in 1961 was supposed to have been the end of Les's Spurs career but he continued to battle for a place and helped the club win the FA Cup in 1962 and the European Cup Winners' Cup in 1963, even if he did not appear in either final. He remained at Spurs until 1965 when he left to join QPR, winning a League Cup winner's medal in 1967.

His son Clive was born in Stepney on 20th May 1961 (two weeks after Spurs had completed the double) and also played for QPR and Spurs, beginning his career at Loftus Road and arriving at White Hart Lane via Arsenal, Crystal Palace and QPR a second time. He is best known for his exploits during the 1986-87 season when he rattled in 49 League and Cup goals, although all he

as a spell as kicker for American football side London Monarchs!

Cousin Paul Allen was born at Avely in Essex on 28th August 1962 and became the youngest player to appear in an FA Cup final when he helped West Ham overcome Arsenal in 1980. He joined Spurs in June 1985 for £400,000 and appeared in two FA Cup finals whilst with the club, collecting a runners-up medal in 1987 and a second winner's medal in 1991. He left Spurs for Southampton in 1993 and later played for Luton, Stoke and Swindon before hanging up his boots.

had to show for his efforts was a runners-up medal in the FA Cup, to go with a similar medal from the 1982 final for QPR against Spurs. Clive later played for Bordeaux, Manchester City, Chelsea, West Ham, Millwall and Carlisle as well

OPPOSITE Les Allen

ABOVE Clive Allen scores during the FA Cup Final against Coventry, 1987

LEFT Paul Allen in action against Arsenal at White Hart Lane, 1988

Archibald

BORN IN GLASGOW ON 27TH September 1956 Steve made his name with Alex Ferguson's Aberdeen side, helping them win two Scottish League Cups and the Scottish championship before a £800,000 move to Spurs in May 1980. He developed an extremely successful partnership with fellow newcomer Garth Crooks and appeared in four finals for the club in the space of four years, collecting winner's medals in the FA Cup in 1981 and 1982 and the UEFA Cup in 1984 and a runners-up medal in the 1982 League Cup. The 1982 League Cup was the only final he scored in, but he did net a total of 97 goals in 216 first team appearances for the club.

A breakdown in his relationship with manager Keith Burkinshaw during the 1983-84 season, which ultimately affected his relationship with his team-mates, saw him sold to Barcelona for £1.25 million in the summer of 1984 (although Burkinshaw had already left the club) where he would go on to win a Spanish championship medal in 1985 and a runners-up medal in the European Cup a year later. After a loan spell with Blackburn Steve returned to Scotland to play for Hibernian, later turning out for Espanol, St Mirren, Reading, Ayr United and Fulham before turning to management with East Fife.

Ardiles

BORN IN CORDOBA ON 3RD AUGUST 1952 Ossie impressed the watching world with his performances for Argentina during the 1978 World Cup and there was speculation that he might be one of the players heading for Spain after the tournament that Argentina won. The announcement that he had signed for Spurs, along with compatriot Ricky Villa in a £700,000 deal in July 1978 caused a major sensation. Although both players took a while to settle into the Spurs midfield, both would have a major impact on the club's fortunes over the next few years. Light on his feet and able to thread the ball with amazing accuracy, Ossie was a major factor in helping the club win major honours at the turn of the decade and brought out the best in Glenn Hoddle.

After helping the club lift the FA Cup in 1981 and overcome Leicester City in the following year's semi-final, Ossie headed back to Argentina to report for World Cup duty. The outbreak of the Falklands conflict caused him to go on a loan deal with Paris St Germain at the start of the 1982-83 season, but after

things didn't work out for him he returned to Spurs in December 1982. A broken leg sustained in his fourth match back seemed to signal that the end of his

ABOVE Ossie Ardiles in action against Liverpool, 1987

ABOVE Ossie Ardiles shields the ball from David Rocastle of Arsenal, 1987

RIGHT Ossie Ardiles kisses the FA Cup trophy after Tottenham Hotspur's 3-2 win over Manchester City in the FA Cup Final replay

Spurs career was approaching but he recovered sufficiently to help the club win the UEFA Cup in 1984. Awarded a benefit match against Inter Milan in 1986 but still suffering from a succession of injuries, Ossie surprised everyone by bouncing back to his best the following season, helping Spurs reach the FA Cup final in 1987.

He finally left Spurs in 1988 for Blackburn on loan before being released and finished his playing career with QPR and Swindon. Ossie then turned to management and in 1993 returned to White Hart Lane with Steve Perryman as his assistant, but his time in charge was not a success and he was relieved of his position in November 1994.

Arsenal

ALTHOUGH SPURS PLAYED ARSENAL for the first time in 1887 and the Gunners can lay claim to being responsible for Spurs' move to White Hart Lane (a friendly fixture between the two sides at Spurs' old ground at Northumberland Park on Good Friday 1898 attracted a capacity crowd of 14,000, with 80 of these perched on top of the roof of the refreshment stand which subsequently collapsed!), the two did not become major rivals until 1913. Even then it was not the result of a clash on the field but the arrival of Arsenal at Highbury in North London that caused the initial rumpus.

Arsenal fans delight in pointing out that they have also won the League title at White Hart Lane as many times as Spurs (two apiece), but it is a fact of North London football that periods of Spurs success have coincided with Arsenal being in the doldrums and vice versa – only once did the two clubs lift major honours in the same year, 1991, with Arsenal finishing League champions and Spurs collecting the FA Cup after beating their nearest rivals in the semi-final. And whilst the two sides have never contested a major final, seven clashes at the semi final stage have seen Arsenal win five of the ties, although Spurs gained suitable revenge with a 5-1 victory in the Carling Cup in 2007-08.

BELOW Celebrations, after victory over Arsenal, 2008

ABOVE Tempers flare in the Premiership match between Tottenham Hotspur and Arsenal, Nov 1999. Spurs won 2-1

COMPETITION	P	W	D	L	F	A
Premiership	32	5	14	13	32	47
Football League	110	40	24	46	158	168
FA Cup	5	2	0	3	5	7
League Cup	11	3	3	5	15	15
Other Leagues	14	6	3	5	25	18
Other Cups	11	4	3	4	14	16
Wartime	36	14	9	13	61	55

Attendances

These figures are Spurs' best and worst attendances at White Hart Lane.

TOP FIVE

75,038	v Sunderland (FA Cup)	5/3/1938
71,913	v Preston North End (FA Cup)	6/3/1937
71,853	v West Bromwich Albion (FA Cup)	24/1/1948
70,882	v Manchester United (Division 1)	22/8/1951
70,347	v Bolton Wanderers (FA Cup)	16/2/1935

BEST

League	v Manchester United	22/8/1951	**70,882**
FA Cup	v Sunderland	5/3/1938	**75,038**
League Cup	v Arsenal	4/12/1968	**55,923**
Europe	v Benfica	5/4/1962	**64,447**

WORST

League	v Sunderland	19/12/1914	**5,000**
FA Cup	v Sunderland	9/1/1915	**16,859**
League Cup	v Barnsley	8/10/1986	**12,299**
Europe	v Grasshopper Club Zurich	3/10/1975	**18,105**

Baker

BORN IN HAMPSTEAD IN LONDON on 10th December 1931 Peter Baker joined Spurs as an amateur from Enfield in June 1949 and was upgraded to the professional ranks in October 1952. Initially understudy to Alf Ramsey, Peter made his Spurs debut during the 1952-53 season when Alf was away on England duty. The arrival of Maurice Norman, who was originally signed as a full-back, threatened Peter's prospects at the club, but when called upon he performed so well that Maurice was forced to switch to centre-half in order to gain his place in the side. Peter broke into the side on a more regular basis during the 1956-57 season and formed a particularly effective full-back partnership with Ron Henry, the only other player from Spurs' double winning side that had not cost a huge transfer fee.

Peter collected winner's medals from the FA Cup in 1961 and 1962, the League in 1961 and the European Cup Winners' Cup in 1963 and was seen, at least by his team-mates, as something of an unsung hero. He was unfortunate in that he was unable to displace Jimmy Armfield from the England side and was thus, along with Les Allen, the only member of the double side not to win international recognition. Peter remained at Spurs until May 1965 when his contract was cancelled and he moved to South Africa to play for Durban City.

Berbatov

THE ACQUISITION OF STRIKER Dimitar Berbatov from Bayer Leverkusen in the summer of 2006 was seen as further evidence of Spurs' awakening as a major force in the English game, for Dimitar was pursued by a number of rivals, including those who could offer almost regular Champions League football. Born in Blagoevgradin Bulgaria on 30th January 1981, the son of a former professional player, Dimitar played for the local side Pirin Blagoevgrad before being spotted by legendary scout Dimitar Penev and snapped up by CSKA Sofia at the age of 17. His tally of 26 goals in just 49 appearances, helping the club win the Bulgarian Cup in 1999, should have made him something of a hero, but a certain section of the crowd singled him out for particular abuse when CSKA lost the League title to rivals Levski. Although he contemplated giving up football, he eventually moved on to Bayer Leverkusen in January 2001.

Whilst goals proved a little more difficult to come by during his early days in Germany, Dimitar did help the club reach the final of the Champions League and came on in the 38th minute as a replacement for Thomas Brdaric in the final. His breakthrough season came in 2003-04, when he netted 16 League

ABOVE Dimitar Berbatov in action at White Hart Lane, May 2007

goals, and a year later bettered that tally with 20, also scoring five goals in Leverkusen's European campaign that term. Such form had many of Europe's top sides running the rule over him, and Dimitar did not disappoint either, netting 21 League goals and three cup goals during the 2005-06 season. In May 2006 Spurs swooped to pay £10.9 million to bring him to White Hart Lane, the costli-

est Bulgarian player in history (not for nothing has he won the Bulgarian Player of the Year award on three occasions).

After taking a while to adjust to the Premiership, Dimitar began doing the job he was brought in to do – netting a hugely impressive 46 goals in 99 first team appearances, including the all-important equaliser in the Carling Cup Final against Chelsea in 2008.

Blanchflower

DANNY BLANCHFLOWER WAS ONE of the greatest players to wear the white shirt of Spurs, as influential off the pitch as he was on it and perhaps the finest captain the club has ever had. Born in Belfast on 10th February 1926 he had a fairly uneventful career with Barnsley and Aston Villa, although he was noted as being a good attacking wing-half and became the subject of a tug of war between Spurs and Arsenal for his signature in October 1954. Spurs offered £2,000 more than Arsenal's ceiling of £28,000 and secured perhaps the one player who ultimately made the double possible.

Although he clashed at times with his later managers, first Jimmy Anderson and then Bill Nicholson, it was always for the right reasons, such as wanting to change tactics and even positioning during matches in an effort to win every game. His cultured and cool play, coupled with his slick passing, propelled Spurs up the table and, after going close to winning the League in 1960, paid dividends the following year as he inspired Spurs to the double. The FA Cup was secured the following year, although Spurs missed out on a second League title (and therefore double double) by virtue of their inability to get the better

BELOW Tottenham Hotspur captain Danny Blanchflower poses with the FA Cup

ABOVE Danny Blanchflower in action

Danny suffered an injury on the way to the European Cup Winners' Cup Final in 1963, one that might have ruled him out of contention, but according to legend Bill Nicholson eventually decided Danny was better with one leg than his proposed replacement John Smith was with two! Danny really made his mark during the pre-match team talk, building his Spurs side up into world beaters – they went out and hammered holders Atletico Madrid 5-1. He retired from playing owing to a recurring knee injury in June 1964 and concentrated on journalism, although there were often rumblings that he might be tempted to come into management. It seemed a likelihood in 1974 when Bill Nicholson retired, for Bill spoke to Danny about taking over and bringing in Johnny Giles as a coach. In the event Danny never applied, the board never contacted him and Spurs were saddled with Terry Neill. Danny did eventually become manager of Chelsea in December 1978 as well as having a spell in charge of the Northern Ireland side, but with limited success. On this basis, perhaps it is just as well he never took over at Spurs; the memories he left at White Hart Lane were all good. He died in Surrey on 9th December 1993.

of Ipswich Town. This was perhaps the only mistake Danny ever made at Spurs, for Bill Nicholson had a plan to combat Ipswich's style that was eventually overruled by Danny. When Bill put his foot down and insisted on playing his way against their Suffolk rivals, Spurs won 5-1!

Brown

A COMMANDING AND athletic goalkeeper Bill first came to prominence with Dundee, helping them win the Scottish League Cup in 1952. Born in Arbroath on 8th October 1931, he was also a more than adequate player outfield, having trials with Scotland schoolboys as a left-winger. It was in goal that his career took off, however, signing with Dundee in September 1949 and being a reserve for the Scottish national side on 22 occasions before collecting his first full cap in 1958. Spurs paid £16,500 to bring him South of the border in June 1959, the last line of a defence that would ultimately enable the club to win the double in 1961. Bill held his place for the victories in the FA Cup and European Cup Winners' Cup over the next two years and also won 24 caps for Scotland during his time at White Hart Lane.

He was seldom challenged as first choice goalkeeper until the arrival of Pat Jennings in 1964, although Bill remained at Spurs until October 1966 when he left to join Northampton Town. Bill later went to Canada to play for Toronto Falcons, eventually settling in the country and working in real estate. He died in Canada on 8th October 2005.

ABOVE Spurs' keeper Bill Brown makes a save

Burkinshaw

EVERY SPURS MANAGER SINCE 1974 has had to live with the fact that his achievements will forever be compared with those accomplished by Bill Nicholson. Of them all since 1974, perhaps only Keith Burkinshaw can hold his head up high and claim that he continued the legacy Bill created. Born in Higham in Yorkshire on 23 June 1935 Keith had a largely undistinguished career as a player but found his true mark as a manager and coach, kicking off this phase in his career with his appointment as player-manager of Workington. A later spell in charge at Scunthorpe was followed by his appointment as coach at Newcastle United in 1968. He was at Newcastle for seven years, helping them reach the FA Cup final in 1974 but was sacked soon after and joined Spurs as coach under Terry Neill. When Neill left the club to take over at Arsenal in July 1976, Keith successfully applied to become the new man at the helm at White Hart Lane. According to the club's then chairman, the board were not that bothered that he didn't have the same kind of profile as other applicants, they were more impressed that he had the ability to work with the players.

Although the club suffered relegation to the Second Division at the end of his first season in charge the board stuck by him and were rewarded with an instant bounce back into the top flight. Keith then pulled off the transfer coup of the century in persuading Ossie Ardiles and Ricky Villa to join the club and, after a couple of seasons consolidating their position in the top flight, mounted a concerted effort to lift some silverware. Winning the FA Cup in 1981 proved to be the launch pad for one of the most entertaining Spurs sides seen for some two decades, and the 1981-82 season deserved better reward than just the FA Cup – the League Cup was lost at Wembley against Liverpool in extra time, Barcelona literally kicked them out of the European Cup Winners' Cup at the semi-final stage and fixture congestion did for them in the League, finally finishing fourth. A similar League placing at the end of the 1982-83 season gave them entry to the UEFA Cup the following season and Spurs quietly made progress in Europe even if their domestic performances were falling away. The announcement that Keith was to leave the club at the end of the season had a galvanising effect on the players who duly delivered the trophy after a heart stopping penalty shoot out against Anderlecht.

Keith's barbed comment that 'there used to be a football club over there' was intended as a dig at a newly installed board who appeared more interested in profit margins and performances on the Stock Exchange than performances on the field. In light of the way the club drifted for the next few years Keith was closer to the truth than even he realised. He later had spells in charge at West Bromwich Albion, was coach to Bahrain and Sporting Lisbon and was director of football at Aberdeen.

BELOW Keith Burkinshaw with the club's two new signings from Argentina, Ricky Villa and Ossie Ardiles

Cameron

JOHN CAMERON IS not a name that will be familiar to many of the club's younger supporters, but those who know enough about Spurs' history will appreciate that without John Cameron, it is doubtful whether Spurs would enjoy their current status, instead being on par with some of the lower level London clubs. It was John, as player-manager, who masterminded the club's victory in the 1901 FA Cup final, still the only occasion that a non-League side has won the FA Cup since the creation of the Football League in 1888.

Born in Ayr on 13th April 1872, John joined Spurs in May 1898 from Everton and was appointed player-manager the following February. John guided the club to the Southern League championship in 1900 and in May of that year bought the player that would ultimately deliver the FA Cup when he arranged the transfer of Alexander 'Sandy' Brown from Portsmouth. Brown would go on to score fifteen goals in the FA Cup that triumphant season, with John also netting a few vital strikes, none more so than the equaliser in the replay of the final itself, from which Spurs went on to beat Sheffield United 3-1.

John resigned as Spurs manager in 1907 (a year before Spurs attained League status, their election being in part down to the kudos that the 1901 cup win had given the club) and went to Germany to coach Dresden FC, subsequently being interned following the outbreak of the First World War. At the end of the hostilities John had a spell in charge of Ayr United before he went into football journalism.

Carling Cup

ALTHOUGH THE LEAGUE CUP (now known as the Carling Cup) was launched during the 1960-61 season, Spurs were one of a handful of clubs that ignored the competition in its formative years, entering for the first time in 1966-67 and then sitting out the following year owing to participation in Europe. The importance of the competition has grown over the years, and over the last decade it has provided Spurs with their only silverware following victories in 1999 and 2008.

After an early exit in 1966-67, Spurs got into their stride in 1968-69, reaching the semi-finals before being beaten over two legs by Arsenal. Two years later Spurs reached the final before beating the then Third Division side Aston Villa 2-0 at Wembley to lift the trophy for the first time and with it ensure European competition in the UEFA Cup. Their reign as holders lasted until the semi-final stage, but Spurs returned to Wembley in 1972-73 and beat Norwich City 1-0 thanks to a goal by substitute Ralph Coates.

Spurs' first defeat in the final came in 1981-82, the competition's first as the Milk Cup, when Liverpool won 3-1 after extra time. There was to be further heartbreak in 1986-87 (beaten by Arsenal in a replay) and 1991-92 (beaten by Nottingham Forest), both of which saw Spurs reach the semi-final stage and no further, but they went one better in 1998-99 with victory over Wimbledon.

In the final (then the Worthington Cup) at Wembley, Spurs beat Leicester City 1-0 in a dour game but collected their first trophy in eight years in the process. They had to wait even longer before next getting their hands on a cup, although they were beaten finalists in 2002, losing 2-1 at the Millennium Stadium to Blackburn Rovers.

In 2006-07 Spurs led 2-0 against Arsenal in the Carling Cup semi-final first leg before being pegged back 2-2 on the night and then losing the second leg. The following season Spurs gained their revenge, drawing 1-1 at the Emirates and enjoying a 5-1 victory at White Hart Lane.

The final, the first back at the new Wembley, saw Spurs come from behind to beat Chelsea 2-1, their first trophy win in nine years and their first under new coach Juande Ramos.

ABOVE Juande Ramos proudly lifts the Carling Cup in 2008

Charity Shield

SPURS HAVE CONTESTED THE FA Charity Shield (now the FA Community Shield) on nine occasions, winning the shield outright on four occasions, sharing it three times and losing just twice. Spurs' first appearance in the match, against West Bromwich Albion in 1920, pitted the First Division champions (WBA) against the Second Division champions. It was not until much later that the League champions automatically played against the FA Cup winners, and Spurs' double success in 1961 meant that they were holders of both trophies. The FA selected a representative eleven to play against Spurs at White Hart Lane, which Spurs won 3-2.

1920	v West Bromwich Albion (H) 0-2
1921	v Burnley (H) 2-0
1951	v Newcastle United (H) 2-1
1961	v FA XI (H) 3-2
1962	v Ipswich Town (A) 5-1
1967	v Manchester United (A) 3-3 *
1981	v Aston Villa (N) 2-2 *
1982	v Liverpool (N) 0-1
1991	v Arsenal (N) 0-0 *

* Shield was shared six months each.

Chivers

BORN IN SOUTHAMPTON ON 27TH April 1945, Martin was so set on becoming a professional footballer. He wrote numerous times to Southampton asking for a trial. He duly impressed and was taken on in September 1962, subsequently linking with Ron Davies and scoring 107 goals in League and Cup competitions in just 189 matches. A £125,000 fee brought him to Spurs in January 1968, with Frank Saul making the opposite journey, and Martin's Spurs' career got off to a blistering start, netting on his debut and hitting two in a cup-tie against Manchester United. A serious injury sidelined him from September 1968 and he struggled for form when he eventually returned, being dropped in to the reserves to try and restore his confidence.

The sale of Jimmy Greaves meant Martin took over as the main goalscorer at the club, linking especially well with Alan Gilzean and going on to help the club win the League Cup in 1971 (he scored both goals in the final against Aston Villa), the UEFA Cup in 1972 (he scored both goals in the first leg of the final against Wolves)

ABOVE Martin Chivers and John McCormick of Crystal Palace dispute a ball

OPPOSITE Garth Crooks in action

and the League Cup again in 1973. First capped by England in February 1971 against Malta, he went on to win 24 caps for his country, netting 13 goals.

Although it was widely reported that he was often at loggerheads with his club manager and assistant, Martin still managed to hit 118 goals in 278 League games and 56 goals in various cup com-

petitions. It was not just his goals that made him a vital member of the side either, for his long throw, usually aimed at Alan Gilzean at the near post, became a key part in the Spurs attacking armoury. Martin was sold to Servette for £80,000 in July 1976, subsequently finishing his career with Norwich City and Brighton & Hove Albion.

Crooks

BORN IN STOKE-ON-TRENT ON 10TH March 1958 Garth was taken on by his local club in 1976 and made his breakthrough into the first team following the transfer of Ian Moores to Spurs. In four years Garth became one of the best strikers in the game, helping Stoke win promotion to the top flight in 1979 and winning his first cap for England Under 21s in November the same year, hitting a hat-trick in the match against Bulgaria.

In July 1980 he was sold to Spurs for £650,000, two months after Spurs had already captured fellow striker Steve Archibald. It was something of a gamble paying such big sums on two strikers, but Keith Burkinshaw's decision was vindicated when the pair hit 36 League and seven FA Cup goals between them in their first season at the club. Such was their impact the FA Cup was won at the end of the season, with Garth netting two of Spurs goals in the semi-final replay against Wolves and a vital equaliser in the final replay against Manchester City. Garth's blistering turn of pace invariably got him around defenders, perhaps best exemplified

with his second goal against Wolves, outstripping the chasing pack to latch onto Glenn Hoddle's through ball.

The FA Cup was retained the following year, with Garth taking on a more important role in the side owing to injury to Archibald and hitting 13 League and three FA Cup goals, including the only strikes in the games against Arsenal and Leeds in the early rounds. A loss of form the following term saw him out on loan to Manchester United for a spell and missing out on the UEFA Cup win in 1983-84, with Garth eventually being sold to West Bromwich Albion for £100,000 in August 1985. A later move to Charlton Athletic also saw Garth struggling for a regular place in the first team, finally retiring through a recurring back problem in November 1990.

Dawson

SOL CAMPBELL'S DEFECTION UP the Seven Sisters Road in 2001 did more than anger legions of Spurs fans; it created a gaping hole in the centre of Spurs' defence that took almost four years to effectively plug. Whilst a number of players were tried alongside Ledley King, none were able to form an effective centre-back partnership until the arrival of Michael Dawson in January 2005.

Born in Leyburn in North Yorkshire on 18th November 1983, Michael joined Nottingham Forest in July 2000 as a trainee, being upgraded to the professional ranks in November the same year. His first team debut came in April 2002, his only appearance that term, but the following season he formed a solid partnership with the veteran Des Walker, helping Forest reach the final of the Play-Offs where they were ultimately beaten by Sheffield United. Whilst Michael's own career was on the ascendancy, collecting the first of his thirteen caps for England at Under 21 level in 2003, Forest were heading in the opposite direction, being relegated to the third tier at the end of the 2004-05 season. By then Michael and his Forest

team-mate Andy Reid had already departed, joining Spurs in a joint deal worth a reported £8 million in January 2005. Given a first team debut away at Liverpool in April that year, he put in the first of countless commanding performances and instantly adhered himself to the Spurs crowd. He would eventually go on to form an exceptional partnership with Ledley King, a partnership that was duly noted by England manager Sven Goran Eriksson and earned Michael a stand by call up to the England World Cup squad for 2006. Although he has yet to make his full England debut, continued solid performances must surely mean this is but a temporary delay.

Seldom beaten in the air, confident on the ground and brave beyond the call of duty, Michael has become a cult hero at White Hart Lane. Dimitar Berbatov, Robbie Keane and Jermain Defoe might get the goals and therefore the plaudits, but the fans appreciate the work that Michael gets through to ensure a Spurs victory. That he should score his first goal for the club against Chelsea in November 2006 only added to his stature.

ABOVE Michael Dawson in action during the Carling Cup Fourth Round match against Port Vale at White Hart Lane, November 2006

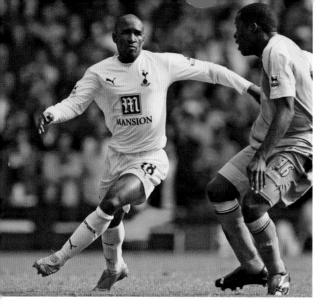

ABOVE Jermain Defoe battles for the ball with Nedum Onouha of Manchester City, May 2007

Defoe

BORN IN BECTON IN LONDON ON 7th October 1982 Jermain was the subject of a tug of war as a youngster, eventually signing as a youth with Charlton Athletic. A controversial switch to West Ham in 1999 cost the Upton Park club substantial compensation, but given the prowess Jermain showed, it was money well spent. He was sent on loan to Bournemouth during the 2000-01 season and scored in ten games in a row, being quickly recalled to West Ham and proving he could score at the higher level, even if not with the same kind of regularity.

Following West Ham's relegation from the Premier League at the end of the 2002-03 season, Jermain slapped in a transfer request (a day after they had been relegated!), which did not endear him to West Ham fans, but he remained at the club to try and help them reclaim their top flight status. As the transfer window was about to close in January 2004, a £7 million fee brought him to White Hart Lane. A goal on his debut and a tally of seven in the final 14 games of the season proved Jermain was a worthwhile acquisition for the club. That goalscoring ability continued into the following term, resulting in 22 goals in all competitions and a call-up for the full England side, with Jermain scoring a vital goal in the away World Cup qualifier against Poland.

The 2005-06 season saw him used more sparingly by Spurs, with coach Martin Jol rotating between Jermain and Robbie Keane as a partner for the more powerfully built Mido. The following campaign saw Jermain still technically third in line, this time behind Berbatov and Keane. Defoe joined Portsmouth in 2008 and made a promising start scoring in his first game.

Dimmock

THE ULTIMATE LOCAL BOY MADE good, Jinking Jimmy Dimmock was born in Edmonton on 5th December 1900 and joined Spurs as an amateur in 1916, being upgraded to the professional ranks in May 1919, despite fierce local competition from Clapton and Arsenal. Injury to Jimmy Chipperfield gave him an almost instant place in the first team and he helped Spurs win the Second Division championship at the end of his first season. The following year saw Jimmy net the most important goal of his career, the only goal of the 1921 FA Cup final against Wolves at Stamford Bridge. On a mud patch of a playing field, Jimmy used both the mud and an opponent's leg to make progress in the Wolves half of the field before firing a low shot that eluded George in the Wolves goal. That winning goal came four days after Jimmy had collected the first of his three full caps for England, in a match where three of his Spurs teammates were also in the England line-up, Arthur Grimsdell, Bert Smith and Bert Bliss.

Jimmy remained at Spurs until 1931, having made 400 appearances, when he left to join Thames, leaving that club when they folded at the end of the 1931-32 season and signing for Clapton Orient. After his playing career came to an end Jimmy worked in the haulage business but continued to live locally. A Tottenham supporter for the whole of his life, Jimmy died in Enfield on 23rd December 1972.

LEFT & BELOW Jimmy Dimmock as depicted on trading cards from his era

Ditchburn

SPURS HAVE BEEN SERVED BY SOME exceptional goalkeepers during their history and Ted Ditchburn belongs in that illustrious company. Born in Gillingham on 24th October 1921 he joined Spurs in 1939, shortly before the outbreak of the Second World War and made his debut for the club in a war-time League match. His proper debut came when normal football was resumed and he would go on to make 418 League appearances for Spurs, a then record. It was his consistency more than anything that made him indispensable, missing only two matches in the seven seasons after the war and racking up 247 consecutive appearances.

His other vital contribution was his realisation that as well as being the last line of defence he was the starting point of any attack, so rather than hoof the ball upfield, he would look to roll the ball out to either of the full-backs, Alf Ramsey or Arthur Willis, who in turn would look to find the half backs; the push and run concept. Whilst manager Arthur Rowe and his team-mates heaped praise on Ted for his actions, Ted was rather more modest, claiming that his 'awful kicking'

LEFT Ted Ditchburn, the Tottenham Hotspur and England goalkeeper

OPPOSITE Ted Ditchburn makes a dramatic save at full stretch from an Arsenal shot during the London derby match, 1950

meant rolling the ball out was a necessity! A member of the side that won the Second and First Division championships in consecutive seasons, Ted won only six caps for England, even though his contemporaries Bert Williams and Gil Merrick won considerably more.

Whilst the England selectors may have had their doubts about Ted, no one at Spurs had any doubts; he was unrivalled as the best English goalkeeper for more than a decade. A broken finger brought his playing career to an end in April 1959 and he went to open a sports outfitters shop in Romford. A regular visitor to White Hart Lane throughout the 1990s, he died on December 26th 2005.

Double

TWO OTHERS ACHIEVED THE FEAT before and three have done it since, but when Spurs won the elusive double in 1960-61, it was considered the football event of the century. Preston North End (in 1889) and Aston Villa (1897) both achieved the feat in Victorian times, but despite a number of near misses, where a team would win the League but fail in the cup final (one or two did it the other way round), no one came close to accomplishing the feat again for more than sixty years. Then Bill Nicholson assembled a side widely reckoned to be the best the country had ever seen, with international players in nine of the eleven positions. The names roll of the tongue with ease; Brown, Baker, Henry, Blanchflower, Norman, Mackay, Jones, Allen, Smith, White and Dyson.

Their accomplishments during the season were little short of amazing – eleven straight victories from the start of the season, 31 League matches won, 115 goals scored – the League was pretty much a certainty from November onwards.

Come January thoughts turned to the second half of the double, the FA Cup. After a tricky 3rd Round encounter with Charlton, Spurs eased past Crewe Alexandra and Aston Villa, overcame Sunderland after a replay and proved too strong for reigning champions Burnley in the semi-final. By the time of the final against Leicester City, Spurs were already League champions and odds on to complete the double. The final itself never lived up to expectations, but goals from Bobby Smith and Terry Dyson in the second half finally won the match. If Spurs had failed to reach their own expectations in the final, then it was only because those expectations were so high.

BELOW The 'double' winning Tottenham Hotspur team with the League Championship and FA Cup trophies to prove it!

Dyson

A DIMINUTIVE WINGER STANDING barely 5' 3", Terry Dyson was born in Malton in Yorkshire on 29th November 1934, the son of a jockey. He signed with Spurs as an amateur in 1954 whilst doing his National Service, turning professional in April the following year. Although he made his first team debut in March 1955, the presence of George Robb and Terry Medwin restricted Terry's first team opportunities during his first two years with the club, and whilst George Robb subsequently retired manager Bill Nicholson went out and bought another winger in the shape of Cliff Jones almost immediately.

Whilst a number of clubs expressed an interest in signing Terry, Bill Nicholson refused to consider selling him, reasoning that he would need an experienced squad for a concerted challenge on the game's top honours. Terry was almost an ever-present during the record breaking double winning season and scored the second of Spurs' two goals in the FA Cup final victory. The following season he was involved in a three way battle with Jones and Medwin for a place in the first team and was unfortunate to miss out when the FA Cup was retained.

Terry was back in the side the following season and had the game of his life in the European Cup Winners' Cup final against Atletico Madrid, scoring two of Spurs goals in the 5-1 win. A broken leg sustained by Terry Medwin meant Terry Dyson retained his place for the 1963-64 season and he remained at Spurs until June 1965 when he was sold to Fulham for a cut-price £5,000.

ABOVE Terry Dyson

Europe

PRIOR TO THE INTRODUCTION OF the European Champions League and the revamping of the UEFA Cup, the two premier European competitions were the European Champion Clubs Cup (to give it its correct title) and the European Cup Winners' Cup. Spurs have competed in the European Cup once (in 1961-62) and the Cup Winners Cup six times (1962-63, 1963-64, 1967-68, 1981-82, 1982-83 and 1991-92).

Spurs' only tilt so far at the European Cup saw them reach the semi-finals, although just after half time of their first match away to Gornik Zabrze they were four goals down, recovering slightly to grab two late strikes that gave them hope for the second leg. It was that second leg that set up future 'glory glory' nights at White Hart Lane as Spurs ran out 8-1 winners and learnt valuable lessons about playing in Europe. Aggregate victories over Feyenoord and Dukla Prague set up a semi-final clash with holders Benfica with the Portuguese side winning the first leg in Lisbon 3-1, although Spurs had two seemingly good goals disallowed for offside. Spurs had reason to feel similarly hard done by after the second leg, where Jimmy Greaves had another strike ruled out and Dave Mackay hit the cross-

ABOVE Bobby Smith scores the opening goal against Benfica in the European Cup semi-final, 1962

BELOW Gary Lineker in action against Hajduk Split in the European Cup Winners' Cup, 1991

bar as the home club did all they could to level the aggregate score. It was not to be, Benfica winning 4-3 on aggregate.

The following season Spurs entered the Cup Winners' Cup and won six and lost only one match on their way to reaching the final in Rotterdam against holders Atletico Madrid of Spain. Although Bill Nicholson was a troubled man before the final, with Mackay out and Blanchflower carrying an injury, his team did him proud, with Jimmy Greaves and Terry Dyson netting two apiece and John White (who was also a late injury scare) hitting the other in a 5-1 victory. The match was closer than the scoreline might suggest, with Spurs surviving a constant onslaught on their goal whilst the score was just 2-1 but weathered the storm and then scored three additional goals to become the first British winners of a major European trophy.

Although Spurs did not make the final again (the competition was disbanded in

1999) they did come close in 1982, reaching the semi-final stage where a particularly brutal Barcelona side kicked their way to a 1-1 draw at White Hart Lane and were little better in the second leg that they won 1-0. Spurs' last appearance in the competition was in 1991-92 when they reached the quarter-finals before going out to Feyenoord.

ABOVE Terry Dyson and Jimmy Greaves show off the European Cup Winners' Cup upon their return to England, after beating Atletico Madrid 5-1 in the final

Competition	Played	Won	Drawn	Lost	For	Against
European Cup	8	4	1	3	21	13
European Cup Winners' Cup	33	20	5	8	65	34
UEFA Cup	78	48	16	13	171	62
Total	**119**	**72**	**22**	**24**	**257**	**109**

FA Cup

PERHAPS THE ONE trophy with which the club are most closely associated, Spurs have one of the best records in the FA Cup, having lifted the trophy on eight occasions out of nine finals. Their first victory came in 1901, when they became the first and so far only non-League side to lift the FA Cup since the formation of the Football League in 1888. That victory required three replays along the way, including one in the final itself, before they finally overcame Sheffield United 3-1 at Burnden Park, Bolton. The final enabled a number of records to be set; the first crowd of more than 100,000, with 114,815 cramming into the Crystal Palace to see the first Final match, the lowest cup final crowd of the 20th century who attended the replay (just 20,470, the crowd being kept low after one of the railway companies refused to issue cheap day return tickets) and goalscoring records for Sandy Brown, who scored in every round and netted a record fifteen goals in the competition.

Spurs next won the cup in 1921 at Stamford Bridge, Jinking Jimmy Dimmock scoring the only goal against

against Burnley 3-1, only the second side to retain the cup in the 20th century.

Spurs were back five years later to beat Chelsea in the first all-London final 2-1 thanks to goals from Jimmy Robertson and Alan Mullery. In 1981, when the year once again ended in a one, Spurs overcame Manchester City in a replay in the 100th FA Cup final, the replay living up to its billing as Spurs won one of the most exciting finals 3-2 thanks to a sublime solo goal from Ricky Villa. Spurs were back again the following year, again needing a replay before seeing off QPR 1-0 through a Glenn Hoddle penalty.

Wolves on a mudheap of a pitch. After the match all the players went to their own respective homes, a celebration banquet not being held until a few weeks later!

There was a gap of forty years before Spurs next made the Final, beating Leicester City 2-0 to complete the double in 1960-61 in what was their first appearance at Wembley. Twelve months later Spurs successfully retained the cup

ABOVE Spurs celebrate with the trophy after winning the FA Cup at Wembley

CENTRE Steve Perryman and Ossie Ardiles lift the cup after beating Manchester City 3-2 in the FA Cup Final replay, 1981

Spurs suffered their first defeat in the FA Cup Final in 1987 when they were beaten 3-2 by Coventry City, but if there was any consolation it came from playing their part in one of the most entertaining finals ever witnessed. Four years later Spurs made amends, coming from behind to beat Nottingham Forest 2-1 in a final most of the neutrals were willing Forest to win, if only because it represented the only trophy manager Brian Clough had not won. Spurs did not allow sentiment to get in their way on the day, then survived the loss of talisman Paul Gascoigne through injury, a penalty miss from the normally reliable Gary Lineker, a perfectly good goal being disallowed to score through Paul Stewart and an own goal from Des Walker. The next time the year ended in a one, 2000-01, Spurs made it as far as the semi-final, their eighteenth appearance in the semi-final, before losing to old foes Arsenal.

Footballer of the Year

THE FOOTBALL WRITERS' ASSOC-
ciation introduced their Footballer of
the Year award in 1948 and the following
players have won the accolade whilst
with Spurs.

1958	Danny Blanchflower
1961	Danny Blanchflower
1973	Pat Jennings
1982	Steve Perryman
1987	Clive Allen
1992	Gary Lineker
1995	Jurgen Klinsmann
1999	David Ginola

The Professional Footballers'
Association introduced their own award
in 1974 and the following Spurs players
have been honoured.

1976	Pat Jennings
1987	Clive Allen
1999	David Ginola

Teddy Sheringham won both awards
in 2001 whilst with Manchester United

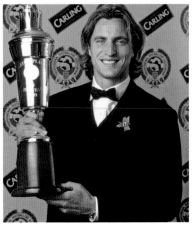

ABOVE Jurgen
Klinsmann holds the
Football Writers' Player
of the Year Award, 1995

LEFT David Ginola was
named 1999 PFA Player
of the Year at the PFA
Awards Ceremony at
the Grosvenor House
Hotel in London

and returned to Spurs in July of that
year. Glenn Hoddle was named Young
Player of the Year in 1980.

Formation

THE HOTSPUR CRICKET CLUB WAS formed in 1880 by pupils from the St John's Middle Class School together with a number of friends from the Tottenham Grammar School. As far as is known the club played only one or two matches, with no record of how they performed having survived. Two years later the boys, who were probably no more than twelve or thirteen years of age, decided to keep their club going through the winter months and therefore adopted football as a sport. There is no official date the football club was formed, but Lindsay Casey, who was the treasurer of the club, duly noted that on 5th September 1882 the newly formed football club received the sum of 5 shillings from the cricket club to assist their formation. Subscriptions were also received on that date from Hamilton Casey (Lindsay's brother), Edward Beaven and Fred Dexter, all of whom paid 6 (old) pence. A day later John Thompson and Bobby Buckle paid a similar sum. The first non-cricket player to join and who therefore had to pay double subscriptions of one shilling

was D Davies. By the end of the month, fourteen boys had paid subscriptions and were therefore members of the Hotspur Football Club. That same month the club bought its first goal posts (2s 6d), flag posts (1 shilling), flags (sixpence), jacks, paint to mark out the pitch, tape and a ball, which probably cost 6 shillings and sixpence, since the club also spent one penny on a stamp on the same day!

Gascoigne

ONE OF THE MOST NATURALLY gifted players of any generation, Paul spent just four years at White Hart Lane but left a lifetime of memories, almost all of them good. Born in Gateshead on 25th May 1967, Paul joined Newcastle United as an apprentice and turned professional in May 1985 having already made his first team debut a month earlier.

By the time he arrived at Spurs for a £2 million fee in July 1988 he had been capped at Under 21 level on thirteen occasions and two months later won the first of his 57 full caps for his country. Another instant favourite with the crowd, Paul had all manner of tricks and touches in his armoury and seemed to take delight in playing the game professionally, a trait that was appreciated by the crowd – there was never a dull moment when Paul Gascoigne was around!

An exceptional World Cup in 1990 that ended in tears after he had been booked in the semi - final and faced a ban had England made the final turned him into a national hero and the following season he was the main reason Spurs reached the FA Cup Final. He scored twice against Oxford in the fourth round, got both against Portsmouth in the fifth and the decisive goal in the sixth round against Notts County. He then underwent an operation for a troublesome stomach muscle but returned for the semi-final against Arsenal and scored one of the greatest free kicks in the his-

ABOVE Paul Gascoigne walks onto the pitch during the Charity Shield match against Arsenal, August 1991

ABOVE Paul Gascoigne darts between Colin Hendry and Peter Reid of Manchester City, Aug 1990

ABOVE RIGHT Paul Gascoigne is given the red card by Referee Vic Callow during a match against Manchester United, Jan 1991

tory of Wembley to set Spurs on their way to a 3-1 win over their arch rivals.

The Final against Nottingham Forest was supposed to have been the match where Paul Gascoigne left an indelible mark. In a sense he did, but it was on the leg of Gary Charles and Paul suffered a serious knee injury that kept him out of the game for a year. It also wrecked a planned move to Italy to sign for Lazio for £8.5 million – by the time the deal

went through in 1992 Spurs had to accept a reduced figure of £5.5 million. His career after that injury, with the possible exception of his time at Rangers, was a major disappointment, with Paul attracting more headlines for his off the field activities than his accomplishments on it. Despite this he was nearly back to his best during the 1996 European Championships, another international tournament that ended with England being beaten at the semi-final stage by Germany.

Gilzean

JIMMY GREAVES AND MARTIN Chivers may have scored more goals, Steve Perryman done more running and Martin Peters supplied more defence splitting passes, but during the end of the 1960s and early 1970s, there was only one King of White Hart Lane – Alan Gilzean. Born in Coupar Angus on 23rd October 1938 Alan first came to prominence with Dundee, helping them win the Scottish League in 1962 and reach the final of the Scottish Cup in 1964.

Although he played in the same position as the man he eventually replaced, Bobby Smith, Alan's style could not have been more different. Where Bobby relied on the direct approach, attacking the ball irrespective of whether there was a defender in the way, Alan was a cultured player with a deft heading ability and the knack of getting into the right position on instinct. He linked especially well with Jimmy Greaves from the moment he arrived at the club for £72,500 in December 1964, with the pair netting more than fifty goals that season. The goals continued to flow for the rest of the decade, although the

ABOVE Alan Gilzean

arrival of Martin Chivers was seen as a threat to Alan's place within the side.

In the event it was Jimmy Greaves who departed, with Alan now becoming as much a supplier of chances for his partner as a finisher in his own right. His heading ability is perhaps one of the

ABOVE Bob Wilson of Arsenal punches clear from Alan Gilzean

RIGHT Alan Gilzean in action

the era and resulted in a good number of goals for the team.

Alan remained at Spurs until the summer of 1974, shortly after the UEFA Cup Final had been lost, so robbing him of the perfect way to end his White Hart Lane career. Alan did return to the ground in November the same year, scoring one of the two goals that beat Red Star Belgrade in his testimonial, with the crowd singing the 'Born is the King' song virtually all night. It can still be heard from time to time today, proof of the affection Spurs fans retain for Alan Gilzean.

abiding memories of the early 1970s, with Spurs going on to add two League Cup and one UEFA Cup victories to the FA Cup Alan had helped win in 1967. His taking up a position on the near post to flick on a Martin Chivers throw-in was a virtual Spurs trademark during

Greaves

EVERY STRIKER WHO HAS managed to net a handful of goals over the last half century automatically gets compared with Jimmy Greaves, usually with the proviso that it is more difficult to score goals today than it was in Jimmy's heyday. The truth is that Jimmy would have scored in any era and probably with the same degree of regularity that he did in the 1960s, since Jimmy scored more often on the field than George Best did off it and with a pre-match ritual that would have today's nutritionists shaking their heads in bemusement. According to Terry Venables, who lived near Jimmy when he signed for Spurs and arranged to travel down to games with him, they stopped at a café where Jimmy ate his way through a full roast dinner, with dessert, and then scored three goals in the afternoon! Jimmy's routine never differed; only the number of goals he scored before his meal was fully digested varied!

Born in East Ham on 20th February 1940, Jimmy was one of the most coveted players as a schoolboy, although as a Spurs fan he was widely expected to

ABOVE Jimmy Greaves runs onto the pitch to cheers from the crowd before the start of the match against Blackpool, 1961

RIGHT Jimmy Greaves in action during a league match

sign for the club when he left school. Illness to manager Arthur Rowe meant Spurs took their eye off Jimmy long enough for Chelsea to snap him up and he went on to score 114 goals for their juniors before signing as a professional. He scored on his debut, against Spurs in 1957 and thus started a streak that he kept up for his entire career – he scored on his debuts for AC Milan, Spurs and West Ham as well as England. Contractually sold to AC Milan in 1960 when the maximum wage was still in effect in England, by the time he flew to Italy the cap had been lifted and the financial lure of going abroad was not as great. Although he proved his goalscoring worth in Italian football he could not settle in the country and was sold to Spurs for £99,999 (Bill Nicholson paid £1 short of £100,000 to avoid burdening Jimmy with the tag of being the first player sold for such a sum) in December 1961.

A hat-trick on his debut set the scene for a phenomenal tally of goals in a Spurs shirt, helping them win the FA Cup twice, in 1962 (he scored once) and 1967 and the European Cup Winners' Cup in 1963 (scored twice). He was to make 322 League appearances for Spurs, scoring 220 goals, made 36 FA Cup appearances (32 goals), eight League Cup appearances (five goals) and eight European appearances (nine goals).

He was just as prolific for England, scoring 44 goals in 57 matches, making him the third highest goalscorer, although both Gary Lineker and Bobby Charlton played considerably more games. It is, of course, the match Jimmy missed that has been constantly brought up over the last forty years – the 1966 World Cup Final, when although he had recovered from an injury sustained in an earlier match, he was overlooked by Alf Ramsey. Some say his career never fully recovered from the disappointment of that day, but League tallies of 25, 23 and

ABOVE Jimmy Greaves sneaks in between Ron Yeats (left) and Tommy Smith (right) of Liverpool, 1965

27 goals in the three seasons after the World Cup would suggest otherwise.

Jimmy was sold to West Ham in 1970 in the same deal that brought Martin Peters to White Hart Lane but retired the following year having netted 357 First Division goals in a glittering career. Fans the length and breadth of the country felt he had retired too early; defenders were glad to see the back of him!

Harmer

AFFECTIONATELY KNOWN as Harmer the Charmer, little Tommy Harmer was one of the most popular players to have turned out for the club. Born in Hackney on 2nd February 1928 Tommy first joined Spurs as an amateur in August 1945 but was not taken on to the professional ranks until three years later, the reason being doubts about his ability to deal with League football when he stood only 5' 6" and weighed just 8 stone 9 pounds.

Those doubts were to accompany his entire career at White Hart Lane as Joe Hulme, Arthur Rowe, Jimmy Anderson and even Bill Nicholson preferred players with greater physical abilities at often crucial times. Despite this Tommy proved himself to be one of the most naturally talented players at the club, able to move into space with the ball with just the merest drop of the shoulders and sending defenders the wrong way.

Having made his debut in September 1951 it was not until 1956 that he got an extended run in the side, although even then there was a sting in the tail – having played a key part in getting Spurs to the FA Cup semi-final against Manchester City, Tommy was dropped from the team at Villa Park and Spurs lost 1-0 with a performance crying out for the creative contributions of The Charmer. Manager Jimmy Anderson relented the following season, installing Tommy as the creative midfielder and Tommy responded by inspiring Spurs to second place in the League. The following season Spurs finished third, Tommy again a major factor in their continued good form, but with the elevation of Bill Nicholson as manager, Tommy's days as a first team regular began to come under threat. The arrival of Dave Mackay and John White, both of whom had the same technical abilities as Tommy but with additional body weight saw them linking with Danny Blanchflower in a revamped midfield and Tommy eventually left Spurs for Watford in October 1960. He later joined Chelsea and scored the vital goal that got them promotion to the First Division in 1963.

Despite all the doubts expressed about his physical attributes, Tommy made 222 appearances for the first team and

didn't let the side down in any one of them. The closest he came to an honour, however, was one England B cap, scant reward to one of the most talented players to have worn the white shirt of Spurs.

Tommy died on Christmas Day 2007.

ABOVE & OPPOSITE
Tommy Harmer

Harry Hotspur

THE NICKNAME OF THE TUDOR hero who ultimately gave the club its unique name, Harry Hotspur was in real life Sir Henry Percy, son of the Earl of Northumberland and a one-time supporter of the deposed and murdered monarch King Richard II. Sir Henry was one of the leaders of the rebel forces who opposed Henry IV and acquired the name Harry Hotspur in recognition of his exploits on the battlefield. He lost his life at the Battle of Shrewsbury in 1403. The relevance to the founders of the Hotspur Cricket Club and later football club was that the Percy family had at one time owned much of the land around Tottenham and the connection was still in evidence when the club was formed, for the club used the Northumberland Arms as a changing room and had their first enclosed ground at Northumberland Park.

The club crest, introduced in 1956, depicts the environment of the club. Bruce Castle is in the top left, the seven trees that were planted at Page Green by the seven sisters of Tottenham (hence the area of Seven Sisters) are top right,

and the two lions rampant were taken from the crest of the Northumberland family, who lived at Black House, later renamed Percy House, which was situated on Tottenham High Road opposite White Hart Lane.

Henry

ALTHOUGH RON HENRY WAS BORN in London on 17th August 1934 his family evacuated to Hertfordshire during the Second World War and he had a spell on the books of Luton as an amateur and playing non-League football with Harpenden and Redbourne. Spurs signed Ron as an amateur in March 1953 and upgraded him to the professional ranks in January 1955, with his League debut coming three months later.

Initially a centre-half he was unable to break in to the first team on a regular basis until brought in to replace the injured Mel Hopkins at full-back during 1957-58. Although Mel eventually reclaimed his position, a subsequent injury sustained on international duty allowed Ron a second bite at the cherry and this time he could not be displaced, appearing in all but one of the next 188 games and collecting a League Championship medal, two FA Cup winner's medals and a European Cup Winners' Cup winner's medal between 1961 and 1963. He also won a cap for England in what was Alf Ramsey's first game in charge, but a 5-1 defeat by France and the continued good form of Ray Wilson meant that was the only major international honour Ron collected.

He was a regular in the side until the 1965-66 season when a cartilage injury forced him initially onto the sidelines and then into the reserves, and although he remained on the club's books until May 1969, he made just one appearance in the League side in his final four years at the club. After retiring Ron concentrated on his garden nursery business in Hertfordshire but continued to assist Spurs on the coaching side.

LEFT Full-back Ron Henry, August 1965

BELOW Ron Henry makes a last ditch tackle on West Bromwich Albion's Bobby Robson

Hoddle

MARTIN CHIVERS FIRST SPOTTED the precocious talents of Glenn Hoddle, observing him playing in a local junior cup final at which Martin had agreed to hand out the trophies. The Hayes born midfielder (his birthdate is 27th October 1957) signed apprentice forms with Spurs in April 1974 and made his League debut as a substitute in August 1975 and his full debut, alongside Martin Chivers, in February 1976 and scored in the 2-1 win at Stoke City.

The following season he became a first team regular and although the season ended with relegation to the Second Division, Glenn had done enough to prove that his was a supreme talent in the making. A key player in the side that bounced back immediately into the First Division, Glenn then found himself sharing midfield duties with the newly arrived Ossie Ardiles and the pair developed an uncanny partnership once Ossie had got to grips with the pace of the English game.

First capped for England in November 1979, Glenn would go on to collect 53 full caps for his country, 44 of these

whilst a Spurs player, but the general consensus was that he was sadly under-used by his country, extended runs in the side only coming when others, less gifted, were either injured or banned. Whilst his country may not have fully appreciated his worth as a player, his club did and Glenn helped steer the club to victories in the FA Cup Final in 1981 and 1982. In the 1981 final it was his free kick that led to the equaliser in the first match, whilst in the replay his delightful lob into space invited Garth Crooks to draw Spurs level at 2-2 against Manchester City before going on to win the cup through Ricky Villa's solo goal. The following year Glenn and Spurs were at their majestic best

ABOVE Glenn Hoddle takes on Arsenal defender David O'Leary during the North London Derby

OPPOSITE Glenn Hoddle passes the ball during the 1982 FA Cup Final against Queens Park Rangers

throughout most of the season, reaching the semi-final of the European Cup Winners' Cup, the final of the League Cup and winning the FA Cup Final as well as finishing fourth in the League. They might have achieved more but for a fixture pile up and it was a case of holding out for some kind of tangible reward in the FA Cup Final, Glenn putting Spurs ahead in the first match and netting the only goal of the replay against QPR from the penalty spot.

Still at his best during the run towards the UEFA Cup Final in 1983-84, Glenn saved perhaps his best performance for the first leg against Feyenoord, giving both Ruud Gullit and Johan Cruyff the runaround as Spurs went into a 4-0 lead. Although Feyenoord netted twice in the second half to give themselves hope for the second leg, a 2-0 Spurs win in Rotterdam ended their interest in the competition. Further visionary passes enabled Spurs to overcome Bayern Munich in the next round, but sadly Glenn suffered an injury in late February 1984 and missed the rest of the run towards the final, apart from a substitutes appearance against Austria Vienna.

In 1986 it was announced that the 1986-87 season would be Glenn's last at

Spurs and he was in superb form as the club headed towards the FA Cup Final once again. A delightful solo goal was his signing off present at White Hart Lane against Oxford United, but at Wembley he was unable to leave the FA Cup trophy as a further momento as Coventry came from behind to win 3-2. He then moved on to Monaco where he won a French League Championship medal before a niggling knee injury began to restrict his appearances. Although he recovered enough to sign for Chelsea on a non-contract basis, he never played for the club and moved on to Swindon as player-manager in March 1991. He returned to Chelsea in June 1993 to become player-manager, taking the club to the FA Cup Final in 1994 where they were beaten by Manchester United.

Glenn was then appointed England manager in the summer of 1996, guiding the national side to the World Cup finals in France in 1998, but revelations about a radio interview coupled with a published account of the World Cup virtually made his position untenable and he resigned in 1999. He returned to club management with Southampton in January 2000 but had an acrimonious split with the club when Spurs invited

him to become their manager in March 2001. He would go on to guide the club to the Final of the Worthington Cup in 2002 but poor League form, coupled with the club's inability to qualify for Europe eventually ended the dream in 2003. He took over at Wolves in December 2004 but left the club at the end of the 2005-06 season.

ABOVE Spurs' Manager Glenn Hoddle encourages his players during the Premiership match against Chelsea

OPPOSITE Glenn Hoddle runs with the ball during the Division One match against Chelsea in 1985

Honours

LEAGUE CHAMPIONS
1951, 1961

LEAGUE RUNNERS-UP
1922, 1952, 1957, 1963

SECOND DIVISION CHAMPIONS
1920, 1950

SECOND DIVISION RUNNERS-UP
1909, 1933

FA CUP WINNERS
1901, 1921, 1961, 1962, 1967, 1981, 1982, 1991

FA CUP RUNNERS-UP
1987

FA CHARITY SHIELD WINNERS
1921, 1951, 1961, 1962, 1967*, 1981*, 1991* (* - shared)

FA CHARITY SHIELD RUNNERS-UP
1920, 1982

LEAGUE CUP WINNERS
1971, 1973, 1999, 2008

LEAGUE CUP RUNNERS-UP
1982, 2002

EUROPEAN CUP SEMI-FINALISTS
1962

EUROPEAN CUP WINNERS' CUP WINNERS
1963

UEFA CUP WINNERS
1972, 1984

UEFA CUP RUNNERS-UP
1974

ANGLO-ITALIAN LEAGUE CUP WINNERS' CUP WINNERS
1971

FA YOUTH CUP WINNERS
1970, 1974, 1990

FA YOUTH CUP RUNNERS-UP
1981, 1995

SOUTHERN LEAGUE CHAMPIONS
1900

Injuries

INJURIES MAY BE PART AND PARCEL of the game and several Spurs players have had their careers ended by injuries sustained whilst playing for the club. Perhaps the worst was that endured by Maurice Norman, a member of the double winning side who suffered a multiple leg fracture whilst playing in a friendly against the Hungarian Select XI in November 1965 and spent two years trying to battle his way back to full fitness. In the summer of 1967 he had to accept defeat and officially retired from the game.

Popular full-back Danny Thomas was the victim of a particularly reckless tackle in a League match against QPR in March 1987 and was stretchered off the field and initially believed to be out for the rest of the season. Although his team-mates dedicated their eventual run to the FA Cup final to their full-back,

ABOVE Injury crippled Maurice Norman's career

Spurs lost at Wembley to Coventry City and Danny was forced to retire from the game in January 1988. He eventually trained to become a physiotherapist!

There are, of course, always exceptions and the one player who best epitomised that was Dave Mackay. He broke a leg playing in the European Cup Winners'

INJURIES

Cup against Manchester United in December 1963 and spent almost a year battling back to fitness, spending hour after hour running up and down the terraces at White Hart Lane to force his way back into the side. The following September, having played one first team friendly and three reserve fixtures, he broke the same leg in a match against Shrewsbury Town Reserves. Typically of Dave, his first words were 'Don't tell Bill', wanting to save his manager from further worries. Dave went back to pounding the terraces in a second attempt to recover full fitness and eventually returned to the first team in August 1965. Not only that, he inspired the side to such an extent he led them to the FA Cup Final in 1967 and collected the trophy after Chelsea had been beaten 2-1.

Quite the most bizarre injury ever suffered by a Spurs player was that encountered by Alan Mullery, who ricked his back whilst cleaning his teeth and was forced to miss out on an England trip to Brazil as a result!

BELOW Dave Mackay (left) and Feyenoord's Cor Veldhoen lie face down on the pitch after a clash of heads left them both unconscious

Internationals

JOHN L JONES HOLDS THE HONOUR of being the first Spurs player to win international recognition, a feat achieved when he represented Wales against Ireland in February 1898. Since then a host of players have earned caps for their countries, with most of the Spurs players who have earned international honours having done so with the traditional Home Countries of England, Scotland, Wales and Northern Ireland and our closest neighbours the Republic of Ireland.

Whilst the launch of the Premiership has seen a slew of international players from all four corners of the globe come to England to play, with more than a fair few plying their trade at White Hart Lane, it should be remembered that Spurs were one of the first clubs to import foreign players, with Ossie Ardiles adding eight caps to his Argentinean tally whilst with the club.

ABOVE LEFT Jermain Defoe in action during the friendly match between England and Uruguay, March 2006

ABOVE Gary Lineker celebrates after scoring the equaliser against West Germany in the World Cup Semi-Final, July 1990

INTERNATIONALS

Since then White Hart Lane has been home to Algerian, American, Belgian, Czech Republic, Canadian, Danish, Dutch, Egyptian, Finnish, German, Icelandic, Israeli, Moroccan, Nigerian, Norwegian, Polish, Portuguese, Romanian, Serbian, South Korean, Swiss and Ukrainian internationals. VIP visitors to White Hart Lane can see a constant reminder of how many international players have turned out for the club, for in the director's Oak Room is a board on which each and every player who has earned international recognition with the club has his name engraved.

On 29th April 1987 in the European Championship qualifier against Turkey in Izmir, Spurs fielded five of the England team – Glenn Hoddle, Steve Hodge, Gary Mabbutt, Clive Allen and Chris Waddle. This was equalled on 1st March 2006 in the friendly against Uruguay at Anfield when Jermain Defoe came on late to join team-mates Paul

Robinson and Michael Carrick, who had been on from the start, Ledley King and Jermaine Jenas, who were brought on at half time. This was the same night that Robbie Keane officially became the new captain of the Republic of Ireland!

WALES TOP FIVE

Caps	Player
41	Cliff Jones
34	Mel Hopkins
32	Ron Burgess
27	Terry Medwin
24	Mike England/Simon Davies

ENGLAND TOP FIVE

Caps	Player
44	Glenn Hoddle
42	Jimmy Greaves
40	Sol Campbell
38	Gary Lineker
36	Chris Waddle

SCOTLAND TOP FIVE

Caps	Player
32	Colin Calderwood
24	Bill Brown
22	Steve Archibald
18	Dave Mackay
18	John White

NORTHERN IRELAND TOP FIVE

Caps	Player
75	Pat Jennings
41	Danny Blanchflower
27	Gerry Armstrong
7	Gerry McMahon
6	Chris McGrath

REPUBLIC OF IRELAND TOP FIVE

Caps	Player
41	Robbie Keane
30	Steven Carr
26	Gary Doherty
24	Joe Kinnear
19	Tony Galvin

ABOVE Paul Robinson in action during the World Cup 2006 Group 6 qualifying match against Austria

ABOVE LEFT Robbie Keane celebrates his goal during the friendly international match between the Republic of Ireland and Sweden, March 2006

Jenas

RIGHT Jermaine Jenas

BELOW Jermaine Jenas in action against SK Slavia Prague in the UEFA Cup, September 2006

BORN IN NOTTINGHAM ON 18th February 1983 Jermaine was taken on by his hometown club as a trainee and signed professional forms in February 2000 having already represented his country at youth level. He quickly established himself as one of the brightest midfield talents in the country and was soon a regular in the England Under 21 side. A £5 million move took him to Newcastle United in February 2002, Jermaine having made just 33 first team appearances for Forest.

Jermaine maintained his progress at St James' Park, earning a call up to the full England side a year later and making his debut in the home friendly against Australia. He was also named PFA Young Player of the Year in 2003, thus capping an eventful twelve months for a player who was barely twenty years of age.

Perhaps at his best in a central midfield role, he found himself being used in a variety of positions whilst at Newcastle, including an emergency appearance at left-back. In the summer of 2005 he said he was fed up with living in a goldfish bowl in Newcastle and was looking for a move elsewhere which subsequently prompted Spurs to pay £7 million for him. His age and attacking instincts made him an ideal target for Spurs and he quickly established an effective partnership with fellow midfield player Michael Carrick. Following Carrick's departure for Manchester United, Jermaine became the creative force in the side, a role he relished.

Jennings

TED DITCHBURN AND BILL Brown were formidable goalkeepers for Spurs, but Pat Jennings proved himself a more than worthy successor and would strongly feature in any debate about who was Spurs' best of all time. Indeed, at the height of his game, Pat Jennings was virtually unrivalled as the best in the world, and I include Gordon Banks in that argument.

Born in Newry on 12th June 1945 Pat played Gaelic football as a youngster which is probably where he acquired his ability to safely handle the ball. He turned to football with Newry Town and was soon a member of the Northern Ireland youth team, representing his country in a youth tournament at Bognor. There he was spotted by former Spurs player and Watford manager Ron Burgess and signed for the Vicarage Road club for £6,000 in May 1963. A little over a year later Bill Nicholson bought him for £27,000, ini-

ABOVE Pat Jennings dives for a ball

tially as cover for Bill Brown, with Pat making his Spurs debut in August 1964 against Sheffield United.

It took Pat just two seasons to permanently dislodge Bill Brown and establish himself as the number one choice, going on to help the club win the FA Cup in 1967. Whilst the rest of the side was re-assembled around him, Pat remained

the one constant for the rest of the decade and into the Seventies, adding further silverware with the League Cup in 1971 and 1973 and the UEFA Cup in 1972. Pat even got himself on the scoresheet too, netting in the FA Charity Shield against Manchester United in 1967 with a long punt intended for Alan Gilzean that actually bounced over Alex Stepney and into the net!

The Football Writers' Association Player of the Year in 1973 and the PFA equivalent in 1976 (Pat claimed he couldn't help but win playing behind the Spurs defence!) Pat could do little to rescue the club from relegation at the end of the 1976-77 season but expressed his desire to stay and help the club battle their way back into the top flight. Unfortunately manager Keith Burkinshaw reasoned that the younger Barry Daines represented a better long term prospect and sold him to Arsenal (of all clubs!) for £45,000 in August 1977. The error was compounded by the fact that Barry never quite lived up to expectations and Pat obviously turned out to be a relative of Peter Pan, getting better with age rather than slowly declining. Suffice to say, Pat added a further FA Cup winner's medal in 1979 and

runners-up medals in 1978 and 1980 together with a runners-up medal in the European Cup Winners' Cup in 1980.

Pat remained at Highbury until the summer of 1985 and then returned to Spurs, supplying cover to Ray Clemence whilst keeping fit in preparation for Northern Ireland's World Cup campaign the following season. He also spent a very brief spell on the books of Everton during the season, just in case anything befell their only experienced goalkeeper (and later Spurs player) Bobby Mimms, in the run up to the FA Cup Final. Pat officially retired at the end of the 1986 World Cup, his last match coming against Brazil, as fitting a way to bow out of the game as any.

The holder of 119 caps for his country and awarded an MBE in 1976 and the OBE in 1987, Pat returned to White Hart Lane again to become specialist goalkeeping coach. It is something of an ironic position for the amenable Irishman for nobody taught Pat how to keep goal during his long and illustrious career; he did everything purely on instinct. But what an instinct, what a goalkeeper!

ABOVE Pat Jennings, makes a brave attempt to save a Sheffield Wednesday goal at White Hart Lane, November 1965

OPPOSITE Pat Jennings roars encouragement to his team-mates, April 1973

Jol

HE'S GOT NO HAIR, but we did'nt care; Martin Jol got Spurs playing the way the fans liked to see their teams play and, more importantly, got them climbing the table. A former player with Den Haag, Bayern Munich and FC Twente, Martin first came to England as a player to join West Bromwich Albion in 1981 and had an early brush with Spurs in the 1981-82 League Cup semi-final which Spurs ultimately won. He then joined Coventry City before returning to Holland to rejoin Den Hagg, being voted Dutch Player of the Year in 1987.

His coaching career began in 1991 with ADO Den Haag and there were spells with Roda JC, Scheveningen, Den Haag and RKC Waalwijk before he accepted the position of assistant coach at Spurs to Jacques Santini. When Santini left after a couple of months Martin was appointed caretaker manager, but an impressive turnaround in the club's fortunes on the field soon had him confirmed as head coach. Spurs narrowly missed out on European football at the end of the 2004-05 season, but Martin and director of football Frank Arnesen and his replacement Damien Comolli identified areas that needed strengthening and have brought in a host of key players, particularly in midfield where Jermaine Jenas and Edgar Davids have bolstered the line-up.

According to reports, Martin was at one time considered for the position of assistant to Sir Alex Ferguson at Manchester United but, when he turned up wearing a tracksuit and T-shirt, coupled with his rather large waistline, it prompted Sir Alex Ferguson to have second thoughts. The sight of Martin patrolling the Spurs touchline, waving to the Park Lane and Paxton Road faithful whenever they sign his name, whilst his side continue their charge for Europe, is proof that appearances can be deceptive.

Jol was sacked in October 2007 after much speculation about the Tottenham hot seat, replaced by Juande Ramos.

Jones

BORN IN SWANSEA ON 7TH FEBRUARY 1935 Cliff Jones began his career with his hometown club in May 1952 and earned the first of his 59 caps for Wales two years later, when aged just 19. Cliff's progress at Swansea was duly noted by other clubs and it cost Spurs £35,000, then a record fee for a winger, to bring the tricky and speedy player to White Hart Lane in February 1958. A member of the Wales side that competed in the World Cup finals that summer, Cliff broke his leg in pre-season training for Spurs that same year and by the time he returned there were three wingers vying for a place in the side – Cliff, Terry Medwin and Terry Dyson.

Cliff's abilities as a goalscorer, with a fair few scored with his head even though he was only 5' 7" tall, was usually enough to give Cliff the nod ahead of his rivals and he was a member of the side that won the double in 1961, the FA Cup in 1962 and the European Cup Winners' Cup in 1963. Cliff also collected a winner's medal in the FA Cup in 1967, albeit as a non-playing substitute in the match against Chelsea at Wembley.

ABOVE Cliff Jones

His sterling services on behalf of Spurs were duly rewarded when he was given a cut price transfer to Fulham in October 1968 after more than ten years as a Spurs player. In 318 League appearances Cliff had netted 135 goals, testament to his worth to the side.

Keane

KEANE

ABOVE RIGHT Robbie Keane celebrates scoring the third goal against Bolton Wanderers at White Hart Lane, February 2007

BELOW Robbie Keane holds up his shirt after a transfer from Leeds to Spurs, August 2002

BORN IN DUBLIN ON 8TH JULY 1980 Robbie was spotted by Wolves as a youngster and taken on as a trainee, joining the professional ranks in July 1997. He quickly established a reputation as one of the best goalscorers outside the Premiership and, after much speculation, was sold to Coventry City for £6 million in August 1999. A year later Internazionale paid £13 million to take him to Italy, but Robbie never fully settled in the country, being loaned to Leeds United and subsequently sold to the Elland Road club for £12 million in May 2001.

Crippling financial problems saw many key players exit Leeds United and Robbie was no exception, signing for Spurs for £7 million in August 2002. He settled in immediately at White Hart Lane

and netted 13 goals in 29 appearances during his first season with the club. He has continued that goalscoring form, getting into double figures in League goals alone and, apart from when he has netted against former clubs, celebrated each and every one with his trademark cartwheel and forward roll!

After seeming to be almost constantly on the move during the early part of his career, Robbie has pledged his willingness to stay and fight for a permanent place within the Spurs side. His most deadly partnership has been with Dimitar Berbatov, with both players netting more than 20 goals during the 2006-07 season as Spurs made progress in three cup competitions. He is also the Republic of Ireland's top goalscorer in history, having netted 32 goals in 79 appearances and becoming captain of the side (he is vice-captain at Spurs).

King

LEDLEY WAS BORN IN BOW IN London on 12th October 1980 and was spotted by Spurs whilst still a youngster, eventually being taken on as a trainee in July 1997. A year later he was upgraded to the professional ranks and made his League debut during the 1998-99 season.

After making steady progress and adding to his tally of first team outings Ledley seemed set to become the permanent defensive partner to Sol Campbell, but Campbell's subsequent defection caused something of a rethink and it is Ledley who has become the senior player in the back four.

First capped by England against Italy in 2002, Ledley's preferred position is as a centre-back but with England having almost an embarrassment of riches in that position he has moved into a holding midfield position in a number of matches. He had played almost half a season in that position for Spurs, so the experience was not a new one.

Quiet and unassuming off the pitch, Ledley is one of the best defenders in the game, seldom beaten in the air and comfortable coming out of defence with the ball, looking to make a telling pass to a colleague. Appointed club captain following the departure of Jamie Redknapp, Ledley is the perfect player for the role, with his confidence in his play an inspiration to his team-mates. He currently has seventeen full caps for England having previously represented his country at Under 16, Under 17, Under 18 and Under 21 level.

ABOVE Ledley King in action at White Hart Lane, May 2007

Kinnear

THE 'PUSH AND RUN' SIDE OF THE 1950s had relied on the ability of the two full-backs to get forward and support the side when they were attacking and it was a policy that Bill Nicholson continued when he became manager. His two full-backs during the latter part of the 1960s and early 70s were among the best in the business, Cyril Knowles at left-back and Joe Kinnear on the right flank. Joe was born in Dublin on 27th December 1947 but moved to England with his family at the age of seven and would go on to represent Watford and Hertfordshire at schoolboy level before signing for St Albans City where he was eventually spotted by Spurs. He joined the club as an amateur in August 1963, turning professional in February 1965 and made his debut in April 1966.

His breakthrough came in February the following year, for regular full-back Phil Beal suffered a broken arm and was ruled out for the rest of the season, with Joe a natural replacement. Joe would therefore go on to help the club win the FA Cup the end of the season and settled in so well at full-back that when

Phil eventually recovered he was unable to displace Joe at full-back, having to slot into a central defensive role.

Joe suffered his own fracture in 1969, breaking a leg in January against Leeds United and spent nearly a year on the sidelines trying to recover. When back to full fitness he found Tony Want and Ray Evans competing for his place in the side, but Joe eventually overcame the opposition and went on to win two League Cup winner's medals (1971 and 1973) and a UEFA Cup winner's medal (in 1972) as well as a runners-up medal in the latter competition in 1974.

Joe remained at White Hart Lane until August 1975 when he signed for Brighton but was forced to retire owing to injury after just a year. He later turned to management, having spells at Doncaster Rovers, Wimbledon, Luton and Nottingham Forest.

ABOVE LEFT Joe Kinnear, 1970

ABOVE RIGHT Joe Kinnear clears the ball from danger, 1968

OPPOSITE Joe Kinnear in 1973

Klinsmann

BERT TRAUTMANN ASIDE, GERMAN players had not been a feature, popular or otherwise, in the Football and Premier Leagues prior to the arrival of Jurgen Klinsmann at White Hart Lane. Whilst he was acknowledged as one of the best strikers in the world, he had also acquired a reputation as something of a diver, quick to fall to the ground inside the penalty area when touched by a defender.

At his first press conference after signing for Spurs, he disarmed the assembled media by politely asking where the nearest diving club was. A few days later, in a move that had been planned with teammate Teddy Sheringham, he celebrated his first goal for the club against Sheffield Wednesday by diving across the field! When later in the same match he was stretchered off after suffering a clash of heads, he received a standing ovation from both sets of supporters!

Born in Goppinggen on 30th July 1964 he arrived at Spurs in the summer of 1994 having become a world star with the likes of Stuttgart, Inter Milan, AS Monaco and his national side, helping the latter win the World Cup in 1990. Indeed, he had been one of the few German successes in 1994 in the USA, but his arrival at Spurs was unforeseen and as big a coup as the signing of Ossie Ardiles and Ricky Villa had been sixteen years earlier. At the time Spurs needed something of a lift, having been hit by a twelve point deduction, a ban from the FA Cup and a huge fine for financial irregularities; the signing of Jurgen (by Ossie Ardiles) certainly provided that lift.

Over the course of the next nine months Jurgen lifted the gloom around

White Hart Lane and, after the points deduction had been overturned and the club reinstated into the FA Cup, he set about trying to help the club pick up some silverware. He came close to achieving that goal, with Spurs making the FA Cup semi-final before being beaten 4-1 by Everton. The highlight had come in the previous round, against Liverpool at Anfield, where Spurs had come from behind to win 2-1, Jurgen netting the winner in the last minute and earning a standing ovation from the Kop at the final whistle.

That seemed to be the standard for the season, with Jurgen proving that the diving reputation counted for nothing; he played the game the way it should be played and was rewarded with 29 goals in 50 appearances for Spurs that season, the highest tally of goals he'd ever achieved. By May 1995 the only person feeling less than enamoured with Jurgen Klinsmann was Spurs chairman Alan Sugar, who saw Jurgen invoke a clause in his contract and sign for his childhood heroes Bayern Munich for a £2 million fee. Jurgen's effect at White Hart Lane was not overlooked however, for he won the FWA Player of the Year award and fully deserved the accolade.

That was not to be the last Spurs fans saw of Jurgen Klinsmann, for in 1998 he returned on loan to help the club battle against relegation and helped himself to four goals against Wimbledon that made Spurs safe. He retired from playing in January 1999 and went to live in the United States, although he was later named manager of the German national side.

BELOW Jurgen Klinsmann breaks past Colin Hendry of Blackburn Rovers, November 1994

Knowles

HUGELY POPULAR DURING AND after his time with the club, Cyril Knowles was one of the most adventurous full-backs ever to pull on the white shirt of Spurs, his exploits made all the more entertaining at a time when the game was drifting into a more defensive pattern and defenders were expected to defend and little else.

Born in Fitzwilliam on 13th July 1944 he had a spell on Manchester United's books whilst he was still playing as a winger, although he was later allowed to leave the club, and also had an unsuccessful trial at Blackpool before drifting into the non-League game. It was Middlesbrough who first recognised that whilst he might not make the grade as a winger, he had all the attributes a full-back needed, including experience of how to combat a winger, and he was signed by the Ayresome Park club in October 1962.

He made only 39 appearances for Middlesbrough, Spurs manager Bill Nicholson seeing him as the ideal replacement for the ageing Peter Baker, Mel Hopkins and Ron Henry, and Cyril joined Spurs in May 1964 for £45,000. He was given his League debut at the start of the following season and would go on to be almost ever-present for the next ten years, collecting caps for England at full and Under-23 level along the way. He was just as vital to Spurs, helping them win the FA Cup in 1967, the League Cup in 1971 and 1973 and the UEFA Cup in 1972, as well as reaching the UEFA Cup Final in 1974. It was the following season, with Spurs battling against relegation that he ensured his place in Spurs folklore, however, netting two goals in a crucial match against Leeds at White Hart Lane to ensure Spurs stayed up.

He even inspired a hit record, with a television commercial for a bread company and the catchphrase 'Nice One Cyril' quickly being adapted by the Spurs fans and turned into a hit record by the Cockerel Chorus which made the Top 20 in 1973! Cyril remained at Spurs until injury forced him into retirement in May 1976 and then turned to coaching and management, serving Doncaster and Middlesbrough as coach and Darlington, Torquay and Hartlepool as manager. In February 1991 it was revealed he was suffering from a serious brain illness and he sadly died in hospital on 31st August 1991. Both Spurs and Hartlepool staged matches in his honour, proof that the affection football fans held for Cyril Knowles reached up and down the country.

LEFT Cyril Knowles, 1973

BELOW Knowles clears the ball off the line at White Hart Lane, 1970

League Positions

Season Ending	Division	Position	P	W	D	L	F	A	Points
1909	2	2nd	38	20	11	7	67	32	51
1910	1	15th	38	11	10	17	53	69	32
1911	1	15th	38	13	6	19	52	63	32
1912	1	12th	38	14	9	15	53	53	37
1913	1	17th	38	12	6	20	45	72	30
1914	1	17th	38	12	10	16	50	62	34
1915	1	20th	38	8	12	18	57	90	28
1920	2	1st	42	32	6	2	102	32	70
1921	1	6th	42	19	9	14	70	48	47
1922	1	2nd	42	21	9	12	65	39	51
1923	1	12th	42	17	7	18	50	38	41
1924	1	15th	42	12	14	16	50	56	38
1925	1	12th	42	15	12	15	52	43	42
1926	1	15th	42	15	9	18	66	79	39
1927	1	13th	42	16	9	17	76	78	41
1928	1	21st	42	15	8	19	74	86	38
1929	2	10th	42	17	9	16	75	81	43
1930	2	12th	42	15	9	18	59	40	39
1931	2	3rd	42	22	7	13	88	55	51
1932	2	8th	42	16	11	15	87	78	43
1933	2	2nd	42	20	15	7	96	51	55
1934	1	3rd	42	21	7	14	79	56	49
1935	1	22nd	42	10	10	22	54	93	30

Season Ending	Division	Position	P	W	D	L	F	A	Points
1936	2	5th	42	18	13	11	91	55	49
1937	2	10th	42	17	9	16	88	66	43
1938	2	5th	42	19	6	17	76	54	44
1939	2	8th	42	19	9	14	67	62	47
1947	2	6th	42	17	14	11	65	53	48
1948	2	8th	42	15	14	13	56	43	44
1949	2	5th	42	17	16	9	72	44	50
1950	2	1st	42	27	7	8	81	35	61
1951	1	1st	42	25	10	7	82	44	60
1952	1	2nd	42	22	9	11	76	51	53
1953	1	10th	42	15	11	16	78	69	41
1954	1	16th	42	16	5	21	65	76	37
1955	1	16th	42	16	8	18	72	73	40
1956	1	18th	42	15	7	20	61	71	37
1957	1	2nd	42	22	12	8	104	56	56
1958	1	3rd	42	21	9	12	93	77	51
1959	1	18th	42	13	10	19	65	95	36
1960	1	3rd	42	21	11	10	86	50	53
1961	1	1st	42	31	4	7	115	55	66
1962	1	3rd	42	21	10	11	88	69	52
1963	1	2nd	42	23	9	10	111	62	55
1964	1	4th	42	22	7	13	97	81	51
1965	1	6th	42	19	7	16	87	71	45
1966	1	8th	42	16	12	14	75	66	44
1967	1	3rd	42	24	8	10	71	48	56
1968	1	7th	42	19	9	14	70	59	47
1969	1	6th	42	14	17	11	61	51	45
1970	1	11th	42	17	9	16	54	55	43
1971	1	3rd	42	19	14	9	54	33	52
1972	1	6th	42	19	13	10	63	42	51
1973	1	8th	42	16	13	13	58	48	45
1974	1	11th	42	14	14	14	45	50	42

ABOVE Les Ferdinand is congratulated by team-mate Steffen Iversen after scoring in the match against Sheffield Wednesday, 1999

LEAGUE POSITIONS

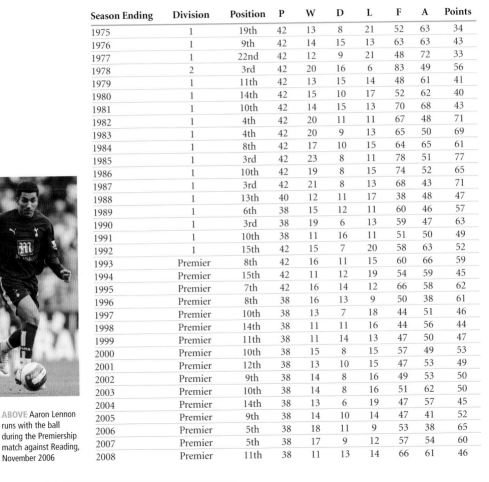

Season Ending	Division	Position	P	W	D	L	F	A	Points
1975	1	19th	42	13	8	21	52	63	34
1976	1	9th	42	14	15	13	63	63	43
1977	1	22nd	42	12	9	21	48	72	33
1978	2	3rd	42	20	16	6	83	49	56
1979	1	11th	42	13	15	14	48	61	41
1980	1	14th	42	15	10	17	52	62	40
1981	1	10th	42	14	15	13	70	68	43
1982	1	4th	42	20	11	11	67	48	71
1983	1	4th	42	20	9	13	65	50	69
1984	1	8th	42	17	10	15	64	65	61
1985	1	3rd	42	23	8	11	78	51	77
1986	1	10th	42	19	8	15	74	52	65
1987	1	3rd	42	21	8	13	68	43	71
1988	1	13th	40	12	11	17	38	48	47
1989	1	6th	38	15	12	11	60	46	57
1990	1	3rd	38	19	6	13	59	47	63
1991	1	10th	38	11	16	11	51	50	49
1992	1	15th	42	15	7	20	58	63	52
1993	Premier	8th	42	16	11	15	60	66	59
1994	Premier	15th	42	11	12	19	54	59	45
1995	Premier	7th	42	16	14	12	66	58	62
1996	Premier	8th	38	16	13	9	50	38	61
1997	Premier	10th	38	13	7	18	44	51	46
1998	Premier	14th	38	11	11	16	44	56	44
1999	Premier	11th	38	11	14	13	47	50	47
2000	Premier	10th	38	15	8	15	57	49	53
2001	Premier	12th	38	13	10	15	47	53	49
2002	Premier	9th	38	14	8	16	49	53	50
2003	Premier	10th	38	14	8	16	51	62	50
2004	Premier	14th	38	13	6	19	47	57	45
2005	Premier	9th	38	14	10	14	47	41	52
2006	Premier	5th	38	18	11	9	53	38	65
2007	Premier	5th	38	17	9	12	57	54	60
2008	Premier	11th	38	11	13	14	66	61	46

ABOVE Aaron Lennon runs with the ball during the Premiership match against Reading, November 2006

Lineker

SPURS FINALLY GOT THEIR MAN second time around in 1989 having previously tried to sign Gary Lineker from Leicester City in 1985. Then the striker, born in Leicester on 30th November 1960, had opted for a move to Everton, helping them finish runners-up in both the League and FA Cup and walking away with both the FWA and PFA Player of the Year awards.

Gary had signed for Leicester as an apprentice and made his first team debut in 1979. Although Leicester were in the Second Division Gary showed a keen eye for goal and his goalscoring exploits soon had bigger clubs paying close attention, prompting a bidding war in 1985. He did even better in the summer of 1986, finishing top goalscorer at the World Cup finals and secured a £2.75 million move to Barcelona upon his return home. A change of manager at the Nou Camp, which saw Terry Venables replaced, left Gary out on the wing, although he did help the club win the European Cup Winners' Cup. By 1989 Venables was manager at White Hart Lane and signed

Gary a second time, expecting him to link up with fellow England internationals Paul Gascoigne and Chris Waddle, but the subsequent sale of Waddle to Marseille ruined that partnership. Gary

ABOVE Lineker in action during a Premiership match against Everton, 1989

and Paul did link well however, and after a hugely successful World Cup campaign in 1990 both players were at the forefront of Spurs' quest for hon-ours the following season. Although Paul Gascoigne got most of the plaudits, Gary grabbed some vital goals in the FA Cup run, none more so than the two in the semi-final against Arsenal that ensured a quick return to Wembley for the Final against Nottingham Forest. There Gary suffered the agony of having a perfectly good goal disallowed for offside and a penalty saved, but Spurs eventually won 2-1 to give Gary his only winner's medal in domestic English football.

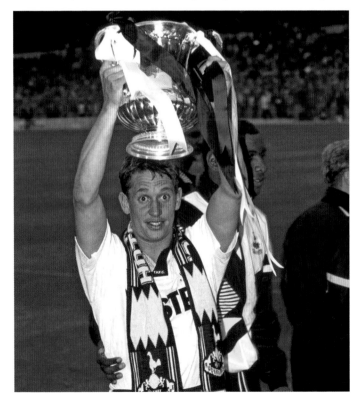

He remained at White Hart Lane until the end of the 1991-92 season when he left for Grampus 8 in the newly formed Japanese League, but a niggling toe injury eventually forced him to retire. He then turned to the media and became a regular presenter of Match of the Day on BBC. He won eighty caps for his country, netting 48 goals and is the second highest goalscorer for England.

Mabbutt

THAT GARY MABBUTT MADE IT AS a professional footballer at all is a remarkable journey, but to have played at the top echelons of the game for so long was virtually superhuman. Early on in his career Gary was diagnosed as being diabetic, a condition that threatened his career before it had even got off the ground, but careful planning and attention to his condition enabled Gary to continue playing the game he loved.

Born in Bristol on 23rd August 1961, the son of former player Ray Mabbutt (Gary's brother Kevin also became a professional), Gary signed with Bristol Rovers in January 1979 and would go on to play in every outfield position during his four years at Eastville. His ability to slot into any position was recognised at international level, Gary earning the first of his Under 21 caps in March 1982 and that summer, whilst other clubs were still considering whether he was able to make the step up a grade or two, Spurs swooped to pay £120,000 to take him to White Hart Lane. To say it was one of the best deals

ABOVE Gary Mabbutt goes for the ball during a Division One match at White Hart Lane, 1990

ABOVE Gary Mabbutt holds the trophy aloft after the FA Cup final win over Nottingham Forest in 1991

Shield and earning the first of his sixteen full caps for England in October the same year.

He helped the club win the UEFA Cup in 1984, replacing the suspended Steve Perryman in the second leg, and a runners-up medal in the 1987 FA Cup final, where he had the misfortune to score both for and against Spurs in the match against Coventry City.

Later appointed club captain at Spurs, it was he who held the FA Cup trophy aloft in 1991 following victory over Nottingham Forest. A succession of injuries, including a broken leg and a horrific facial injury threatened his career from time to time, but Gary kept bouncing back, refusing to let injury halt his career any more than diabetes had done.

Whilst Gary was an inspirational player on the field for Spurs, off it he was considered just as important an influence towards fellow diabetics and was awarded the MBE in 1994. This hugely popular player was released by Spurs at the end of the 1997-98 season having made 619 first team appearances and continues to be an ambassador for the game in general and Spurs in particular.

the club ever did would be something of an understatement, for Gary made rapid progress at the club, making his debut at Wembley in the FA Charity

Mackay

ANY DEBATE ON WHO IS THE greatest player to have played for Spurs would surely include Dave Mackay somewhere along the way, for not only was he extremely talented he was also one of the bravest and toughest players who wore our colours.

Born in Edinburgh on 13th November 1934 he joined Hearts as a part-time professional in April 1952 and made his Scottish League debut during the 1953-54 season. After doing his National Service Dave returned to Tynecastle and helped the club win the Scottish League Cup in 1955, the Scottish FA Cup in 1956 and the Scottish League in 1958, their first Championship since 1897! Not surprisingly, such success on a domestic level led to Dave being capped at Under 23 and full level, representative honours with the Scottish League and recognition as Scotland's Player of the Year in 1958.

Dave was to add one further medal north of the border, helping Hearts to the Scottish League Cup in 1959 before a move south beckoned. Bill Nicholson had originally intended bidding for Mel Charles but for once failed to get his

ABOVE Dave Mackay, 1960

man and instead turned his attentions to Dave, a player he had admired but had felt that Hearts would be reluctant sellers. They had no wish to see Dave leave but a cheque for £30,000 proved persuasive and Dave joined the international all stars being assembled at White Hart Lane in March 1959.

Whilst Dave may have lacked pace, he more than made up for it with his on

ABOVE Dave MacKay training at White Hart Lane, 1959

the field attitude, an aggressive streak kept him within the boundaries of the game's laws but frightened his opponents, which was half of the battle. When it came to outright talent, Dave was up there with the best and would often take part in showmanship skills in training, beating almost all of his team-mates.

It was said that the acquisition of Dave was the final part of the jigsaw that enabled the double to become a reality and Dave certainly played his part in bringing both trophies to White Hart Lane, curtailing his own goalscoring instincts that had netted him eleven goals in 1959-60 in order to better serve the team. At the end of the 1960-61 season therefore Dave had added League Championship and FA Cup winner's medals to those he had won in Scotland and thus became the first player to have won the set both sides of the border.

Dave added a second FA Cup winner's medal in 1962 but was sadly to miss the club's greatest night in Europe through a stomach injury. Worse was to follow the next season as Spurs set about defending the cup, for Dave broke his leg in the match against Manchester United that eventually saw Spurs eliminated. Dave spent almost a year battling to get back to full fitness and then broke the same leg in a match against Shrewsbury Reserves. Whilst lesser men than Dave Mackay might have seen fit to retire at that point, Dave fought back to lead the club to the FA Cup Final in 1967 and proved an inspirational captain, lifting the trophy after Chelsea had been beaten 2-1.

Dave remained at Spurs until July 1968 when he left to join the Derby revolution being carried out by Brian Clough, and not only helped Derby win promotion to the First Division in 1969 but was also named joint Player of the Year with Tony Book by the FWA. Dave later turned to management, taking Derby to the League Championship in 1975 and having a hugely successful spell in Kuwait.

Managers

Manager	Year
Frank Brettell	1898 to 1899
John Cameron	1899 to 1907
Frank Walford *	1907
Fred Kirkham	1907 to 1908
Peter McWilliam	1912 to 1927
Billy Minter	1927 to 1929
Percy Smith	1930 to 1935
Wally Hardinge *	1935
Jack Tresadern	1935 to 1938
Peter McWilliam	1938 to 1942
Arthur Turner	1942 to 1946
Joe Hulme	1946 to 1949
Arthur Rowe	1949 to 1955
Jimmy Anderson *	1955 to 1958
Bill Nicholson	1958 to 1974
Terry Neill	1974 to 1976
Keith Burkinshaw	1976 to 1984
Peter Shreeves	1984 to 1986
David Pleat	1986 to 1987
Trevor Hartley *	1987
Doug Livermore *	1987
Terry Venables	1987 to 1991
Peter Shreeves	1991 to 1992
Doug Livermore +	1992 to 1993
Ossie Ardiles	1993 to 1994
Steve Perryman *	1994
Gerry Francis	1994 to 1997
Chris Hughton *	1997
Christian Gross +	1997 to 1998
David Pleat *	1998
George Graham	1998 to 2001
David Pleat *	2001
Glenn Hoddle	2001 to 2003
David Pleat *	2003 to 2004
Jacques Santini +	2004
Martin Jol +	2004 to 2007
Juande Ramos	2007 to date

* Caretaker manager + Coach

ABOVE LEFT David Pleat signals to his players during the match against Blackburn Rovers, May 2004

ABOVE Spurs manager Gerry Francis, 1996

LEFT George Graham is appointed new manager of Tottenham Hotspur, October 1998

ABOVE Terry Medwin

OPPOSITE Luka
Modric attends a match
to watch his new team

Medwin

BORN IN SWANSEA ON 26TH
September 1932 Terry signed with the
local club in 1946 and became a professional in November 1949. He was used
in all five of the forward positions at
Swansea, including centre-forward
despite the fact that he was only 5' 9"
tall, and by the time he joined Spurs in
April 1956 for £25,000 he was the club's
leading goalscorer.

Terry's own favoured position was as
a right-winger and it was in this berth
that he made his initial impact at White
Hart Lane, flying down the wing with
such poise he soon earned an international recall having been overlooked for
almost three years. A regular in the
Spurs side for some four years, the
arrival of Cliff Jones and the battling
qualities of Terry Dyson left Bill
Nicholson with a selection problem
going into the double season. Whilst
Terry Dyson made more appearances
on the right (Cliff was switched to the
left), Terry Medwin still made his presence felt in the 15 appearances he made.
Terry (Medwin) got some consolation
the following year when he was a member of the side that retained the FA Cup
at Wembley against Burnley.

Terry made just two appearances in
what would become the successful quest
for the European Cup Winners' Cup in
1962-63 and then in the post-season
tour of South Africa broke his leg in a
friendly against an Invitation XI.
Although he spent a year trying to
regain his fitness, he admitted defeat in
the summer of 1964 and retired from
playing, subsequently becoming manager of non-League Enfield.

Modric

WHERE MANY DITHERED AND waited, Spurs swooped, paying a club record equalling fee of £16.5 million to secure the services of Luka Modric for the 2008-09 season. Born in Zadar on 9 September 1985, Luka joined Dinamo Zagreb as a sixteen year old and was sent on loan to Zrinjski Mostar (where he was named Bosnian League Player of the Year during his spell with the club) and Inter Zapresic before returning to Zagreb in 2005.

Over the next three years he established himself as one of the most talented playmakers in the Croatian game, helping the club win the Croatian First League in 2006, 2007 and 2008, the Croatian Super Cup in 2006 and the Croatian Cup in 2007. His performances for Croatia had spread the word on his abilities far beyond his home country, with Luka playing a key part in eliminating England from the European Championships in 2007.

With several leading European clubs pondering on making an offer during the summer of 2008, Spurs swooped in April 2008 to snap him up on a six year contract.

Nicholson

THE MOST IMPORTANT MAN EVER to walk through the doors of White Hart Lane, Bill Nicholson's impact at Spurs can never be understated – as a player he was a vital cog in the push and run side, but everything he achieved as a player was completely overshadowed by his accomplishments as a manager. Certainly the greatest manager Spurs have ever had, he belongs in the same illustrious company as Herbert Chapman, Matt Busby and Bill Shankly as one of the greatest managers the game has ever seen.

Born in Scarbrough on 26th January 1919 Bill spent a short time with the club's nursery side Northfleet before being offered professional forms in August 1938, going on to make his League debut in October the same year. The outbreak of the Second World War the following year put his playing career on hold and Bill spent the war as a PT instructor. At the end of the hostilities he returned to White Hart Lane and, playing at right-half, was a key component in the side that won the Second Division title in 1950 and the First Division Championship a year later. He also won his only full cap for England in 1951 against Portugal, scoring with a header with his first touch after just 19 seconds, the quickest debut goal ever scored by an England player. Although he was named as a reserve on a record 22 occasions (in the days before substitutions) the continued form of Billy Wright prevented Bill from adding to his tally of caps.

Bill retired from playing in 1955 and used his previous experience as a PT instructor to good effect, becoming coach at Spurs and also assisting the England set-up, being coach to the 1958 World Cup squad. Bill was asked to take over as manager of Spurs in October 1958 following the resignation of Jimmy Anderson and, although the club was languishing in the lower reaches of the First Division table, responded with a 10-4 victory over Everton that same day.

It took Bill a while to get the players he wanted and the pattern he desired, but by 1960 everything was in place. After narrowly missing out on the League title in 1960, Spurs made sure of it the following season, winning the title with a record equalling 66 points and lifting the FA Cup after a 2-0 win over Leicester City at Wembley. It was the first double of the 20th century and was won by a side many still claim to be the best the country has ever seen. Spurs should have put their domination beyond any argument the following season with another double, but defeats home and away to Ipswich (managed by former Spurs player Alf Ramsey) when the players dictated the formation cost them the League title. Spurs made no mistake in the FA Cup, beating League runners-up Burnley 3-1 in one of the great finals.

The FA Cup was seen as little more than consolation, however, for the real prize the club craved in 1962 – the European Cup. Although Bill was thorough in his preparation for every game, Europe was a new experience and his side had to recover from going four goals down in Poland against Gornik Zabrze before scoring two vital goals in the first leg and then winning the second leg 8-1. Spurs marched all the way to the semi-final where they faced holders Benfica, but although Spurs could claim refereeing mistakes had cost them two goals in the first leg, Bill was more concerned about

ABOVE Bill Nicholson, February 1954
OPPOSITE Bill Nicholson, 1965

ABOVE A commemoration at White Hart Lane to former Spurs player and manager, Bill Nicholson, who died on 23 October 2004

the mistakes his defence made in conceding three goals. Spurs nearly overcame the 3-1 deficit in the second leg, winning 2-1, having another goal chalked off for offside and hit the bar.

Bill guided Spurs to their first European success in 1963, winning the European Cup Winners' Cup in magnificent style with a 5-1 hammering of holders Atletico Madrid in Rotterdam, although Bill was unusually nervous before the game and it needed the rallying cries of Danny Blanchflower to lift the side.

The retirement of Blanchflower, the death of John White and a broken leg sustained by Dave Mackay ripped the heart out of the double side, but Bill rebuilt, collecting the FA Cup in 1967 by way of a surprise and then had another good side, if not a great one, in place for the turn of the next decade. Victories in the League Cup in 1971 and 1973 and the UEFA Cup in 1972 might not have been the same kind of heights the 1960s side had scaled, but they were still better than a host of other clubs could achieve.

Bill originally intended resigning in 1974 after the UEFA Cup Final, which pitted Spurs against Feyenoord, but against a backdrop of rioting supporters, Spurs slipped to a 4-2 aggregate defeat and Bill put his plans on hold. Four games into the following season Bill resigned, although he did agree to remain in charge until a replacement could be found. When Terry Neill took over, Bill severed his connection with the club and did some scouting for West Ham, but following the appointment of Keith Burkinshaw in 1976, Bill returned to White Hart Lane as consultant.

Bill later became chief scout and could claim credit for uncovering the likes of Graham Roberts, but Bill being Bill, he never claimed credit for anything. Everything he did during his entire working life was done for the benefit of Tottenham Hotspur Football Club. In 1991 he was named Club President, a fitting position for someone who had done so much to put the club on the football map. Awarded the OBE in 1975, there is still a campaign to get him the knighthood his achievements deserved. Bill Nicholson, so long a fixture of White Hart Lane, died on 23rd October 2004 after a short illness.

Norman

A SOLID AND DEPENDABLE CENTRE-back, Maurice was born in Mulbarton in Norfolk on 8th May 1934 and joined Norwich City in September 1952. Originally a full-back, he made his first team debut three years later and made 35 appearances for the Canaries before he was identified as the perfect replacement for the ageing Alf Ramsey in the Spurs back line and joined the club in November 1955.

An injury sustained in September 1956 kept him out of the Spurs side for half a dozen matches and by the time he recovered, Peter Baker had done so well as his replacement Maurice was unable to reclaim his full-back position. Fortunately there was an opening for a centre-half and with Maurice's abilities in the air, he proved the ideal man for the job.

Maurice really shone at the start of the decade, winning most if not all of his individual battles with the opposing centre-forwards and helped the club win the League title and FA Cup in 1961 and retaining the FA Cup the following year. That same season he was awarded the first of his 23 caps for England and seemed set for an extended run in the team. There was further glory for Spurs and Maurice in 1963, the club winning the European Cup Winners' Cup, and whilst the side went through a number of changes in 1964 and 1965, with virtually the entire midfield requiring replacements, Maurice still remained. A horrific multi-fracture sustained in a friendly against a Hungarian Select XI brought Maurice's career to a shuddering halt and despite enduring a number of operations, he never played again and was forced to retire in the summer of 1967.

Overseas Tours

ABOVE RIGHT Anthony Gardner fights for the ball during the Peace Cup Final, July 2005

BELOW Tottenham Hotspur players celebrate their win at the Peace Cup Final, July 2005

SINCE UNDERTAKING THEIR FIRST overseas tour in 1905, a continental tour that took in Austria, Hungary and Czechoslovakia and included two exhibition matches against Everton, Spurs have visited many different countries around the world and won friends and fans in all of them.

Spurs also played two exhibition matches against Everton during their tour of Argentina and Uruguay in 1909, a tour that saw one of the Spurs players win a fancy dress competition on the voyage home dressed as Long John Silver, with the ship's parrot used as a prop. The club was presented with the parrot as a souvenir of the voyage and, according to legend, the parrot died when Arsenal were voted into the First Division in 1919 in place of Spurs!

Spurs made their first trip to Germany in 1911 and, encouraged by their reception, made repeat visits in 1912 and 1914, but by the time they arrived for the latter tour, the First World War was barely months away and there was considerable hostility towards the Spurs team during their time in the country. Indeed, so hostile was their reception club chairman Charles Roberts stated that no Spurs team would ever visit the country again whilst he remained as chairman. Charles died in 1943 and Spurs finally returned to Germany in 1950.

In 2005 Spurs broke new ground by visiting South Korea for the first time in order to participate in the Peace Cup, a competition they ultimately won by overcoming Boca Juniors, Sundowners, Real Sociedad and Lyon in the final.

Perryman

ONE OF THE MOST LOYAL SERVANTS to have worn the Spurs shirt, Steve Perryman holds most of the appearance records for the club, having been on the club's books for almost twenty years. Born in Ealing on 21st December 1951 Steve was another youngster much coveted by the London clubs and after representing London and England Schools opted to sign as an apprentice at Spurs in July 1967. He was upgraded to the professional ranks in January 1969 and made his League debut in September the same year against Sunderland.

Used initially as something of a midfield terrier, Steve quickly slotted into the midfield alongside the likes of Martin Peters and Alan Mullery, winning the ball in a tackle and laying it off short for his team-mates. He could also be relied upon to get among the goalscorers and scored at least one goal a season during his time at White Hart Lane.

The younger member of the side that won the League Cup in 1971 and 1973, Steve's most vital games came in the UEFA Cup in 1972, where he scored both crucial goals at home to AC Milan in the semi-final as Spurs recovered from going a goal behind to winning the home leg 2-1. Although he didn't score in the final, it was his ability to win his midfield battles that proved the key to Spurs winning the trophy.

With the eventual departure of Alan Mullery and Martin Peters, Steve was

ABOVE Steve Perryman in action, 1981

ABOVE Steve Perryman is tracked by Arsenal's John Hollins, 1980

in 1978 and then winning the FA Cup in 1981 and 1982. That latter season was something of a personal triumph for Steve, for he was named FWA Player of the Year and awarded his solitary cap for England in the friendly against Iceland in June.

There was near glory for Steve in the 1984 UEFA Cup as he helped the club reach the final, but an unfortunate second booking received in the first leg of the final against Anderlecht kept him out of the second leg at White Hart Lane, with Graham Roberts collecting the trophy after Spurs' penalty shoot out victory (the players had wanted Steve to collect the trophy on their behalf but were refused permission by UEFA). According to legend Ossie Ardiles gave him his winner's medal in recognition of the part Steve had played in getting the club to the final in the first place.

He remained a Spurs player until the summer of 1986 and had spells as a player with Oxford United and Brentford before turning to management and coaching, including a time back at White Hart Lane with Ossie Ardiles as assistant. The pair continued their partnership in Japan and Steve later served Exeter City as director of football.

named club captain and moved into a more defensive position, often playing at full-back behind the likes of Glenn Hoddle. He quickly adapted to his new role and was the inspiration behind the club regaining their First Division status

Peters

ENGLAND MANAGER ALF RAMSEY once claimed Martin Peters was ten years ahead of his time, an attempt at a compliment that at times returned to almost haunt Martin, for he was never allowed to forget the tag. Born in Plaistow on 8th November 1943 he joined West Ham in May 1959 as an apprentice having already earned representative honours with Dagenham, London, Essex and England at schoolboy level.

Martin was upgraded to the professional ranks in November 1960 and made his League debut in April 1962, going on to add an England Under 23 level cap to his name before the year was out. A member of the West Ham side that won the FA Cup in 1964 and the European Cup Winners' Cup a year later, Martin just missed out on a hat-trick of winner's medals when West Ham finished runners-up in the League Cup in 1966. He received more than adequate compensation that summer, for having made his England debut in May 1966, he retained his place for the World Cup finals and scored England's second goal

ABOVE Martin Peters, 1970

in the 4-2 win over West Germany.

With his West Ham team-mates Bobby Moore having skippered the side and Geoff Hurst scoring a hat-trick, the contributions of Martin Peters tended to get overlooked, which, coupled with

ABOVE Peters in action

rediscover the form that had made him such a key player during the middle of the decade.

In fact Spurs fans probably got to see the best of Martin Peters, for his ability to ghost into space, deliver crucial passes to teammates and weigh in with goals himself made him a key part of the side that won the League Cup in 1971 and 1973 and the UEFA Cup in 1972, being captain when they lifted the League Cup in 1973.

Martin remained at Spurs until March 1975 when he was surprisingly sold to Norwich City for £60,000, the figure ridiculously low for a player who would add over 200 appearances for the Canaries to the 287 he had racked up at Spurs and more than 300 for West Ham. Awarded an MBE in 1978 he finished his playing career at Sheffield United before briefly switching to coaching and management, ending his football career when Sheffield United were relegated into the Fourth Division. He then went into the motor insurance business with Geoff Hurst and was later appointed to the board of directors at Spurs.

Alf Ramsey's comments made him somewhat unsettled. Eventually he moved to Spurs in a £200,000 deal in March 1970 with Jimmy Greaves making the opposite journey, and began to

Quotes

'Football is not really about winning, or goals, or saves, or supporters…it's about glory. It's about doing things in style, doing them with a flourish; it's about going out to beat the other lot, not waiting for them to die of boredom; it's about dreaming of the glory that the Double brought.'
DANNY BLANCHFLOWER

'It's better to fail aiming high than to succeed aiming low. And we of Spurs have set our sights very high, so high in fact that even failure will have in it an echo of glory.'
BILL NICHOLSON

'Over there all the attackers attack and the defenders defend. That means all your midfield players attack as well. Ossie (Ardiles) and Ricky (Villa) didn't know the meaning of the word defend when they first came here.'
KEITH BURKINSHAW after Spurs had lost 7-0 at Anfield against Liverpool.

'However long you look at football and think of all the great teams, you won't find any who could knock it about better than Tottenham did today. They are not necessarily a great team, they might not win the Championship because they are a bit vulnerable when they haven't got the ball, but they are great for the game.'
JOHN BOND on the 1982 side

'I fell in love with the club and it is still my favourite. I was made very welcome there by everyone and the fans were always marvellous. There is always a place in my heart for Tottingham Hotspurs.'
OSSIE ARDILES

'The biggest regret of my whole football career was leaving White Hart Lane in 1970…My interest in football weakened after that. I was heartbroken.'
JIMMY GREAVES

'There used to be a football club over there.' KEITH BURKINSHAW

Ramos

LIKE MANY FORMER PLAYERS whose careers were brought to an abrupt end owing to injury, Juande Ramos has made sure his managerial and coaching career has more than compensated. A midfield player for a number of Spanish sides, his career was halted with a knee injury at the age of 28. He then turned to coaching, taking CD Logrones and Rayo Vallecano to promotion from the Spanish Segunda Division.

He arrived on the world map with his exploits at Sevilla FC, lifting the club up the League and winning the UEFA Cup in 2005-06 and again the following year (beating Spurs along the way) as well as domestic success with the Copa Del Ray and Supercopa de Espana in 2007. Whilst the victories were

undoubtedly important, the style his team played, earned equal plaudits and rumours abounded during the summer of 2007 that he had been approached by Manchester City, who had a managerial vacancy, and Spurs, who did not, with a view to trying his luck in the Premier League.

He opted to remain in Spain, but in October 2007 Spurs returned looking for a replacement for the recently departed Martin Jol and a dizzying offer secured the services of a coach who placed as much emphasis on the right diet as he did tactical abilities. Spurs were languishing near the bottom of the table when he arrived; whilst the League form continued in the same uneven manner that had brought Jol's reign to an end, progress was made in the various cup competitions, culminating in a glorious day at Wembley when Spurs ended their nine year wait for a trophy with victory in the Carling Cup.

With a summer to prepare his troops for the coming endeavours, the 2008-09 season will give a clearer indication of Juande Ramos' abilities. He is, however, already off to a perfect start – just ask the thousands at Wembley that February afternoon.

Ramsey

ALTHOUGH HE WOULD FIND greater fame as England manager, it is never forgotten at Spurs that Alf Ramsey was one of the key players in the great push and run side and often the starting point of the attack. Born in Dagenham on 22nd January 1920 Alf was spotted by Portsmouth and signed as an amateur in 1940, although he never got to play for the Fratton Park club, switching to Southampton after starring against them in an Army match. His initial contract at The Dell was also as an amateur, turning professional in 1943.

Alf moved to White Hart Lane in 1949 for the then record fee for a full-back of £21,000, for although he was already an England international (he would go on to win 32 caps for his country) he reasoned he stood a better chance of improving his career at Spurs. His arrival at Spurs completed the great push and run side and it was his runs into space, looking for throw outs from Ted Ditchburn that set the whole side moving. Second Division Champions in 1950, Spurs won the League title the following year and finished runners-up

in 1952. FA Cup glory was nearly achieved in 1953 when Spurs reached the semi-final but an uncustomary mistake from Alf in underhitting a back pass allowed Blackpool to take the game and ultimately win the Final against Bolton.

Upon retiring as a player Alf took up a position as part-time manager of Eton Manor and was then appointed manager at Ipswich Town in 1955. He steered the club to the Third Division South Championship in 1957, the Second Division Championship in 1961 and the League title in 1962, taking a relatively unknown side to the pinnacle of English League football ostensibly because no one knew how to combat their tactics.

RIGHT Alf Ramsey, England manager, 1970

He was appointed England manager in October 1962, the first official manager, and insisted on doing things his way. He made the proud boast that England would win the World Cup in 1966 and delivered on his promise, although it meant further tactical changes during the course of the competition before he developed what became known as the wingless wonders. It was claimed that as a full-back he had never been keen on wingers anyway!

Alf remained England manager until 1974 when he was relieved of the position after England had failed to make the 1974 World Cup Finals. He later served Birmingham City as a director and had spells as caretaker manager at St Andrews without ever actively pursuing a full time position back within the game. After suffering a stroke in 1998 Alf was admitted to a Suffolk nursing home and died from prostrate cancer on 28th April 1999.

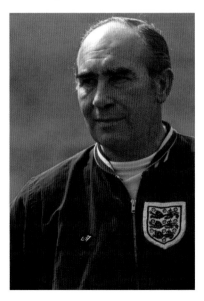

Records

Record victory
13-2 v Crewe Alexandra, FA Cup fourth round replay 3/2/1960

Record defeat
0-7 v Liverpool, Division One, 2/9/1978

Most League points
77 in Division One in 1984-85 (under three points for a win), 70 points in Division Two in 1919-20 (under two points for a win)

Most League goals
115 in Division One, 1960-61

Highest League scorer in a season
Jimmy Greaves, 37 in Division One, 1962-63

Most League goals in total aggregate
Jimmy Greaves, 220, 1961-70

Most League appearances
Steve Perryman, 655, 1969-86

Most capped player
Pat Jennings, 74 caps for Northern Ireland

Record transfer fee received
£18 million (reported) from Manchester United for Michael Carrick, August 2006

Record transfer fee paid
£16.5 million to Charlton Athletic for Darren Bent, July 2007, £16.5 million to Dinamo Zagreb for Luka Modric, April 2008.

LEFT Spurs' top goal scorer, Jimmy Greaves

BELOW Previous record transfer fee player Sergei Rebrov celebrates his goal against Fulham, 2001

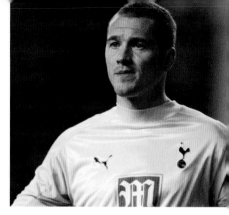

Robinson

CONTINUING THE LONG LINE of exceptional goalkeepers to have kept goal for Spurs, Paul Robinson was widely acclaimed to be the best in England and one of the best in Europe when barely out of his teens. Since goalkeepers tend to get better with age, there is no limit to what he can achieve in the future.

Born in Beverley on 15th October 1979 he joined Leeds United straight from school and made his debut for the club against Chelsea in 1998. Paul was immediately seen as a strong challenger to England international Nigel Martyn and eventually replaced him as first choice, prompting Nigel to move to Everton in an attempt to revive his own career. Paul also collected his first cap for England in February 2003 against Australia and following one mistake too many from David James, became England's first choice in September 2004.

By then Paul was a Spurs player, having joined the club in May 2004 for a fee of £1.5 million. Spurs had previously bid for Paul in January the same year with a view to loaning him back to the financially troubled Leeds United for the rest of the season, but Premiership rules forbade the loan and Spurs had to wait an extra four months before finally getting their man.

His exceptional positional sense, shot-stopping ability, his agility and his quick and direct clearances to attacking teammates make him the country's best goalkeeper by a long way. He has also got himself on the scoresheet before now, coming upfield late in a League Cup tie that Leeds were losing and netting the equaliser. He then performed extra heroics in the penalty shoot out to turn a near defeat into victory. In March 2007 against Watford he added to that tally, hitting the ball more than 80 yards and seeing the ball bounce over rival England goalkeeper Ben Foster for Spurs' second in a 3-1 victory.

RIGHT Paul Robinson, Spurs' No 1

BELOW Paul Robinson dives for the ball in the match against Watford at White Hart Lane, March 2007

Rowe

BUT FOR THE SUCCESS OF BILL Nicholson's Double winners ten years later, the 'push and run' side guided by Arthur Rowe would be revered as the best Spurs side ever assembled. Like Bill, Arthur gave Spurs exceptional service as both a player and manager and both players collected one cap for their country when their performances deserved more.

Born in London on 1st September 1906 Arthur joined Spurs as an amateur in 1923 and was farmed out to nursery clubs Cheshunt and Northfleet before returning to White Hart Lane to sign professional forms in May 1929. Although he appeared in a London FA Charity match in 1930 he had to wait until the following year to make his League debut but once in the side, Arthur was there to stay.

A member of the side that won promotion back into the First Division in 1933, Arthur was capped for England against France in December the same year and had helped Spurs towards the top of the League (they were ultimately to finish third at the end of their first season back in the top flight) when he

suffered a knee injury. Although not necessarily career threatening, it was the start of a series of injuries that affected Arthur and was enough to keep him out of the side long enough for Spurs to lose their First Division status in 1935.

ABOVE Arthur Rowe in action for Spurs, 1934

ABOVE Arthur Rowe, manager of Tottenham Hotspur, 1949

Arthur was in and out of the side thereafter and in April 1939 released on a free transfer. Rather than slip down the divisions Arthur opted to pursue a coaching career and accepted an assignment in Hungary. The sudden outbreak of the Second World War hastened his departure back to England and during the hostilities he coached the Army side. When war ended Arthur took over as manager of Chelmsford City and guided them to the Southern League title at the end of his first season in charge. His success with extremely limited resources at Chelmsford impressed the board at Spurs and he was appointed manager in 1949.

Although most of the side that would win back to back Championships was already in place by the time Arthur arrived at White Hart Lane (the acquisition of Alf Ramsey was down to Arthur), it was Arthur who gave them the style. He didn't particularly like the phrase 'push and run', preferring instead to outline the way his team played with a series of sayings – 'make it simple, make it quick' and 'when not in possession get into position'. Spurs romped to the Second Division title in 1950 and the following year, after a sticky start, made progress up the table to finally lift the First Division title with a victory against Sheffield Wednesday.

Runners up in 1952 and a place in the semi-final of the FA Cup in 1953 effectively saw the end of Spurs' domination in the early 1950s and the pressures of trying to keep Spurs at the top proved too much of a strain for Arthur. He suffered a nervous breakdown in 1954 and ended his connection with Spurs, although he later recovered and scouted for West Bromwich Albion, and was assistant manager of Crystal Palace before taking over and guiding them out of the Fourth Division. He later served Orient and Millwall as well as serving on various League committees.

Arthur Rowe, one of the greatest managers Spurs ever had, inspirer and teacher of Alf Ramsey and Bill Nicholson, two of the greatest managers England has ever seen, died on 8th November 1993.

Sheringham

SPURS PAID £2.1 MILLION TO SIGN Teddy Sheringham in September 1992 when they could have had him for considerably less than that ten years previously – he had a trial with the club when he was setting out to become a professional player and was unsuccessful!

Born in Highams Park on 2nd April 1966 Teddy also had a trial at Orient and trained with Crystal Palace before finally getting himself signed to Millwall, becoming a professional in January 1984. After a spell on loan to Aldershot Teddy became a regular at Millwall and scored 93 goals in 220 appearances, helping them win the Second Division title in 1988. He was sold to Nottingham Forest in July 1991 for £2 million and would help them reach the finals of the Simod Cup and League Cup in his first season, the latter at the expense of Spurs.

His move to White Hart Lane was something of a surprise, but Teddy soon slotted into the side and helped Spurs to the FA Cup semi-final in his first season as well as collecting the first of his 51 caps for England. Although never the quickest of strikers, his footballing brain allied with his sharp reflexes ensured he was more often in the right place at the right time – the old adage of the first two yards being in your head could have been written with Teddy Sheringham in mind.

Although Teddy enjoyed a certain degree of success with England, helping them to the European Championship

ABOVE Teddy in action against West Ham United, September 2002

ABOVE Teddy Sheringham is challenged by Chris Coleman of Blackburn, August 1996

a bigger club, prompting Manchester United to pay £3.5 million for his signature. After a barren first season, he then won all of the game's top honours – three League titles (in successive seasons), the FA Cup and the European Champions League, the latter two coming in the record-breaking 1998-99 season when United won the treble and Teddy scored in both finals. The only honour that eluded him that season was the Worthington Cup, where United were beaten by the eventual winners – Spurs!

Released on a free transfer in 2001 Teddy returned to White Hart Lane and had two seasons back at Spurs, helping them to the final of the Worthington Cup in 2002. He later helped both Portsmouth and West Ham back into the Premiership and continues to play today, one of the oldest outfield players still in action.

semi-finals in 1996, Spurs' inability to break into the top echelons of the domestic scene became the source of much frustration for Teddy and in July 1997 he announced his desire to move to

Smith

A BUSTLING CENTRE-FORWARD IN the old-fashioned sense, Bobby Smith terrorised defences across the whole of Europe but, as his fifteen caps for England would testify, was an awful lot more skilful than ever given credit for.

Born in Langdale on 22nd February 1933 Bobby joined Chelsea as an amateur in 1948 and became a professional in May 1950. Although he made his debut whilst still only 17 he was never a regular, being unable to unseat Roy Bentley from the side. Spurs offered £16,000 for him in December 1955 but Bobby originally refused the move, changing his mind after a stern lecture from Chelsea manager Ted Drake!

The move proved to be his making, for Spurs built their attack around his strengths and were rewarded by Bobby equalling the club goalscoring record with 36 strikes during the 1957-58 season. Although only 5' 10" tall, his very presence worried defenders and he learnt to use every ounce of his 12st 11lbs weight to further intimidate them into making mistakes. In the double winning season of 1960-61 Bobby hit 28

goals, also grabbing one of the goals that won the FA Cup. He repeated the feat in the cup final the following year, whilst a year later he grabbed four during Spurs' march towards lifting the European Cup Winners' Cup.

In May 1964 he was transferred to Brighton for £5,000 and added a Fourth Division Championship medal to his honours list, netting 18 goals during the 1964-65 season. He never got the chance to play in the Third Division however as he was sacked before the start of the season owing to a series of newspaper comments. That probably summed Bobby Smith up perfectly – uncompromising both on and off the field, he spoke and played in a simplistic manner but achieved great results.

ABOVE Bobby Smith (right) clashes with Morrall (centre) and Nigel Sims of Aston Villa, September 1960

The Top Ten

LEAGUE APPEARANCES

Rank	Player	Apps
1	Steve Perryman	655
2	Gary Mabbutt	477
3	Pat Jennings	472
4	Ted Ditchburn	418
5	Cyril Knowles	401
6	Jimmy Dimmock	400
7	Glenn Hoddle	377
8	Maurice Norman	357
9	Alan Gilzean	343
10	Danny Blanchflower	337

ALL COMPETITIONS

Rank	Player	Apps
1	Steve Perryman	865
2	Gary Mabbutt	620
3	Pat Jennings	596
4	Glenn Hoddle	492
5	Cyril Knowles	484
6	Jimmy Dimmock	460
7	Ted Ditchburn	457
8	Tom Morris	428
9	Phil Beal	425
10	Sandy Tait	421

LEAGUE SCORERS

Rank	Player	Goals
1	Jimmy Greaves	220
2	Bobby Smith	176
3	Cliff Jones	135
4	George Hunt	124
5	Martin Chivers	118
6	Len Duquemin	114
7	Les Bennett	102
8	Jimmy Dimmock	100
9	Billy Minter	95
10	Bert Bliss/Alan Gilzean/Taffy O'Callaghan	93

OVERALL SCORERS

Rank	Player	Goals
1	Jimmy Greaves	268
2	Bobby Smith	215
3	Martin Chivers	181
4	Cliff Jones	159
5	George Hunt	138
6	Len Duquemin	134
7	Alan Gilzean	133
8	Les Bennett	118
9	Jimmy Dimmock	112
10	Glenn Hoddle	110

UEFA Cup

SPURS HAVE COMPETED IN THE UEFA Cup on seven occasions and won the trophy twice and on the other four occasions reached the final, semi-final, the quarter-finals twice and second round. Spurs first tilt at the trophy came in the inaugural season of 1971-72 when they qualified as League Cup winners and saw off the challenge of Keflavik, FC Nantes, Rapid Bucharest, Unizale Textile Arad and AC Milan to make the final. The semi-final clash against AC Milan was particularly hard, Spurs having to come from a goal down in the home leg before winning 2-1 thanks to two goals from Steve Perryman. In the return an Alan Mullery thunderbolt gave Spurs a two goal aggregate lead and although Milan pulled one back, Spurs held on to win overall.

Their reward after trekking all around Europe was a two-legged final against Wolverhampton Wanderers, the only occasion a major European Cup Final has been contested by two English sides, and two goals from Martin Chivers away from home gave Spurs a 2-1 win in the first leg. Alan Mullery again got on the scoresheet in the second leg, being knocked out in the process of heading home from a free kick, but he recovered to inspire Spurs to hold on for a 3-2 aggregate win and their second

European trophy after success in the Cup Winners' Cup in 1963.

The following season saw the trophy remain in England, but it was Spurs' semi-final conquerors Liverpool who got their hands on it. Spurs won the League Cup again that season and went back into the UEFA Cup in 1973-74. Although their League form was poor throughout the campaign, they seemed able to lift themselves for Europe, beat-

ing Grasshoppers Zurich, Aberdeen, Dinamo Tbilisi, FC Cologne and Lokomotiv Leipzig to make the final against Feyenoord. At home Spurs twice had the lead but were pegged back in the closing moments to finish all square at 2-2, whilst the second leg saw rioting by Spurs fans as their team went down 2-0. The rioting earned Spurs a ban from Europe, but as they didn't qualify for the next eight years it didn't really seem to matter.

Spurs qualified for the UEFA Cup again in 1983-84 after two seasons in the Cup Winners' Cup and used their

ABOVE Steve Archibald wins the ball from Georges Grun of Anderlecht during the UEFA Cup Final second leg match at White Hart Lane, 1984

CENTRE The Spurs team celebrate after their victory in the UEFA Cup Final against Anderlecht, May 1984

growing experience to good effect to see off Drogheda, Feyenoord (home and away victories), most famously Bayern Munich, Austria Vienna and Hadjuk Split to reach the final against holders Anderlecht, although it had looked as though their opponents were to be Nottingham Forest, who led 2-0 after the first leg but lost the second 3-0 in a match where it was later proved that Anderlecht had bribed the match officials. Spurs earned a more than credible 1-1 draw in Belgium, Anderlecht equalising in the closing moments. The second leg, which had the additional emotional tie of being manager Keith Burkinshaw's last match in charge, did not go according to plan, Anderlecht taking the lead and seemingly capable of holding on to it until Graham Roberts burst through to fire home the

equaliser. No goals in extra time set up the heart-stopping penalty shoot out, a series of penalty kicks that made a hero out of Tony Parks.

Spurs defence of the trophy the following season got off to a good start, with SC Braga, Club Brugge and Bohemians Prague seen off with little or no difficulty. That brought Real Madrid to White Hart Lane for the quarter-final first leg, where Spurs were finally beaten at home for the first and still only time in European competition by a Steve Perryman own goal. Steve didn't have any better luck in the second leg either, getting sent off, but Spurs also had a perfectly good goal disallowed for supposed offside, even though the Real Madrid players weren't appealing.

Spurs' next appearance in the competition came in 1999-2000 when they went out in the second round against Kaiserslautern. Spurs returned to the competition during the 2006-07, overcoming Slavia Prague with 1-0 victories home and away, even though their opponents were the seeded side, to make the group stages. They then recorded a 100% record in their four matches, beating Besiktas, Club Brugge, Bayer Leverkusen and Dinamo Bucarest to top the group. Initially drawn against Feyenoord, Spurs were awarded a bye into the next round when the Dutch club were thrown out of the competition for the behaviour of their fans in an earlier match. After beating Braga home and away to set a new British record of eight consecutive victories in European competition, Spurs faced UEFA Cup holders Seville in the quarter-finals. Despite taking the lead after only two minutes of the first leg in Seville, Spurs were beaten 2-1 (the equaliser coming from a ridiculously awarded penalty) on the pitch whilst their fans were being beaten in the stands by the police. A dreadful eight-minute spell in the second leg saw them concede two goals and left them a mountain to climb. Two goals inside a minute raised their hopes on the hour mark, but a resilient Seville defence and a catalogue of misses meant they went out 4-3 on aggregate.

Spurs qualified for the 2007-08 competition with another fifth place in the Premier League. After seeing off Famagusta in the qualifying round, Spurs were expected to breeze through their group, but a home defeat by Getafe signalled the end of Martin Jol's reign as Head Coach.

His replacement Juande Ramos steered Spurs through the group and into the knockout stages, but after seeing off Slavia Prague over two legs, they lost on penalties 6-5 to PSV Eindhoven after both sides had won their away matches 1-0 in the Round of 16. Spurs will be after further progress in the 2008-09 season, having earned qualification through victory in the Carling Cup.

ABOVE Dimitar Berbatov gets past José Luis Martí of Sevilla during the UEFA Cup quarter-final second leg match at White Hart Lane, April 2007

Venables

BORN IN BETHNAL GREEN on 6th January 1943 Terry became the only player to have been capped for England at every possible level – schoolboy, youth, amateur, Under 23 and full – all of which were achieved whilst associated with Chelsea. He was sold to Spurs in May 1966 and would collect an FA Cup winner's medal in 1967 against Chelsea. However, he was never able to fully settle at Spurs and moved on to QPR in June 1979. After five years at Loftus Road Terry moved on to Crystal Palace but retired soon after and joined the coaching staff. He then turned to management, turning Crystal Palace in to the Team of the Eighties and later managing QPR and Barcelona.

He was sacked at Barcelona in 1987, soon after Spurs had parted company with David Pleat and after his business dealings were sorted out, Terry took over at White Hart Lane. A number of high profile players came in during his time, including Gary Lineker, Paul Gascoigne and Paul Stewart, but equally one or two of the club's better players were allowed to leave, most notably Chris Waddle. Despite this and against a backdrop of growing financial problems Terry led Spurs to victory in the 1991 FA Cup and helped put together a supposed dream ticket of himself and mogul Alan Sugar to rescue the club.

A fallout between the two saw Terry sacked in 1993, a sacking that was confirmed despite a protracted legal challenge. Aside from a successful spell as England coach, Terry's career since leaving White Hart Lane has mirrored his two spells at Spurs, promising more than it delivered.

Villa

JUST AS JIMMY DIMMOCK HAD done sixty years early, Ricky Villa made himself a cult hero at White Hart Lane thanks to one goal in an FA Cup Final. Since most readers are too young to have appreciated Jimmy Dimmock (including the writer!), one can only imagine the adulation he was afforded at the time, but if it is anything like that of Ricky Villa, it must have been something special – Ricky still gets a rapturous reception at White Hart Lane, twenty five years after he scored that goal.

Born in Buenos Aires on 18th August 1952 Ricky had played for Quilmes and Athletico Tucuman before signing with Racing Club and was a member of the successful Argentinean squad for the 1978 World Cup. Keith Burkinshaw heard through contacts that Ossie Ardiles, who played in the final, might be available for transfer to England and journeyed to Argentina to get his man, but on arrival was told that Ricky might also be available. A combined fee of £700,000 brought the two players to White Hart Lane, with Ossie slotting in almost immediately alongside Glenn Hoddle in midfield.

ABOVE Ricky Villa runs with the ball during the match against Aston Villa, September 1981

Although Ricky scored on his first team debut against Nottingham Forest, he took longer to adjust to the team's rhythm and was in and out of the side as Keith Burkinshaw tried to find a formation that could accommodate all his midfield players. It was the FA Cup of 1980-81 that made Ricky's reputation, but it will surprise many people to learn that he played in the third round and

was then absent until Spurs reached the semi-final. Largely anonymous in the first match, he scored a cracking third goal in the replay against Wolves at Highbury to confirm Spurs' appearance in the Final.

Ricky had an even quieter match at Wembley against Manchester City, with Burkinshaw substituting him for Garry Brooke in an attempt to rescue a game Spurs were trailing 1-0. Rather than join the bench, Ricky set off on a lonely walk towards the dressing room, got close to the entrance and then changed his mind and walked back to the bench. There were those, his captain among them, who thought Ricky's actions deserved some retribution, such as leaving him out of the replay, but Keith reckoned he wouldn't play that badly again and named an unchanged side. It turned out to be an inspired decision, for Ricky scored the opening goal to set Spurs on their way. With fifteen minutes left and the score delicately poised at 2-2, Ricky collected the ball from Tony Galvin wide on the left hand wing. Ricky cut inside, took the ball past Caton, around Ranson, cut back across Reid and avoided a desperate lunge from the recovering Caton and the onrushing goalkeeper Joe Corrigan to sweep the ball home for the winner. Ricky's celebration run after the goal was almost as long as his run to score and took him past as many Spurs players as his earlier run had City ones!

Although Ricky helped the club reach the Final of the League Cup and the FA Cup the following season, he only figured as a substitute in the former, the outbreak of the Falklands War just before the FA Cup semi-final being deemed too political an issue to allow for an Argentinean to play in the Final. Which was a pity – both matches against QPR cried out for that one moment of inspiration that Ricky had produced twelve months earlier. Ricky remained at Spurs until June 1983 when he went to play in America, but Spurs got one further glimpse of their hero when he turned out for the club in Tony Galvin's testimonial in 1987. All night the crowd were willing Tony to pass the ball to Ricky whenever they were out near the left wing…

Waddle

BORN IN HEPWORTH ON 14TH December 1960 Chris Waddle came into the professional game relatively late, having had several unsuccessful trials as a youngster and going on to play part-time for Tow Low Town whilst working in a sausage seasoning factory. After another unsuccessful trial he was given one final try and managed to impress Newcastle United enough to earn a contract. He made up for lost time at Newcastle, benefiting from manager Arthur Cox's tuition and playing alongside professionals such as Kevin Keegan and Peter Beardsley, going on to earn selection for England at Under 21 level.

By March 1985 he had broken into the full England side and would go on to win 65 caps for his country, a remarkable figure for a player who didn't come into the professional game until in his

ABOVE Chris Waddle in action against Coventry City in the FA Cup Final, 1987

twenties. His form for Newcastle prompted a raid by Spurs, who paid £650,000 to take the tricky winger to White Hart Lane in July 1985. He linked especially well with Glenn Hoddle, both on and off the field (the pair were to enjoy a Top 20 hit record as a pair and

ABOVE Chris Waddle fends off a tackle from Sheffield Wednesday's Carlton Palmer, 1989

usual wide position in the side for a more vital central role, eventually becoming the main playmaker alongside the mercurial talents of Paul Gascoigne. The arrival of Gary Lineker as striker was supposed to herald a bright new beginning for Spurs but within a matter of weeks Chris was himself the target for French club Marseille and eventually joined in July 1989 for £4.5 million. Twice a French League Champion and a runner up in the European Cup, Chris returned to England with Sheffield Wednesday in 1992. He later played for Bradford City and Sunderland and was player manager of Burnley before joining Torquay United.

Chris Waddle didn't look much like a footballer when he strode out onto the field, with his hunched shoulders and habit of looking almost constantly towards the ground, but in full flight he could weave his way around almost any defender and was one of the few bright spots during a particularly depressive time for Spurs towards the end of the 1980s. The one question that will forever remain unanswered is how good he, Paul Gascoigne and Gary Lineker could have been for Spurs – they certainly produced the goods for England.

also a Top 40 hit as part of a group – Spurs), particularly during the 1986-87 season when they were the key parts of the famed five man midfield that provided lone striker Clive Allen with the ammunition to score 49 goals.

Following Glenn Hoddle's transfer to France and Monaco, Chris swapped his

White

DANNY BLANCHFLOWER AND DAVE Mackay received more of the plaudits during the double season, but the role played by John White in securing the two trophies can never be underestimated. It was impossible to miss Dave as he bossed the midfield, or the delightful passing abilities of Danny, but most of John's work went unnoticed – the run into space to give a team-mate an option, the sudden arrival in attack to lend support or just the constant movement that made him such a vital player.

Born in Musselburgh on 28th April 1937 John began his professional career with Alloa Athletic in August 1956 and two years later moved on to Falkirk for £3,000. Within a year he had broken into the Scottish national side, prompting attention from clubs in England. Bill Nicholson initially dithered over whether to sign him, and it was only the glowing reports from Spurs international players who had come up against him that convinced him John might be a worthwhile acquisition. His doubts about his stamina were put to rest when he learnt John had won representative awards for cross-country – a £20,000 fee brought him to White Hart Lane in October 1959.

Whilst Spurs fans took a while to fully appreciate his abilities, his team-mates had no doubts and he became just as vital to Spurs in the three-year success-laden spell as Mackay and Blanchflower. He was equally important to Scotland, going on to receive 18 caps for his country during his time with the club.

Away from football his big passion was golf and it was this passion that was to result in his untimely death. Scheduled to play a round with another player on 21st July 1964, John arrived early just as a violent thunderstorm broke out. Sheltering under a tree to escape the rain, John was struck by lightning and died instantly. Although Spurs had already suffered the loss of Danny Blanchflower (retired) and Dave Mackay (broken leg), the loss of John White and the manner in which it occurred was one even Bill Nicholson took time to get over. John White was such a talent, Bill never quite managed to replace him.

ABOVE John White, 1964

White Hart Lane

ABOVE The Tottenham Hotspur cockerel stands proudly on top of the East Stand at White Hart Lane

THE WORLD FAMOUS HOME OF THE Spurs, White Hart Lane has been Tottenham Hotspur's ground since 1899. The club had originally played at Tottenham Marshes until the need for an enclosed ground, where supporters could be charged an admission fee, resulted in a move to Northumberland Park in 1888.

Spurs soon outgrew the Park, matters coming to a head with the visit of Woolwich Arsenal in 1898 when 14,000 packed into the ground and there were a number of injuries sustained when the roof of a refreshment hut collapsed through having too many people on it! The incident prompted two Tottenham responses; firstly the club became a limited liability corporation and secondly chairman Charles Roberts began searching for another ground, one that would allow future development.

According to legend, Charles Roberts heard from an apprentice that a new football club was going to start playing on the vacant space at the rear of the

White Hart public house just off Tottenham High Road and less than a mile from Spurs' own ground at Northumberland Park. Roberts hurried over to the White Hart to speak to the landlord to ascertain the situation. It turned out there was no club, although the landlord was keen to start one since

ABOVE Inside the stadium at White Hart Lane

he had previously had a tenancy near Millwall and done good trade on a Saturday when Millwall were at home. Whilst the landlord had not got his idea off the ground, he was willing to allow Charles Roberts to negotiate with his landlords Charrington & Co for a leasehold on the White Hart site, reasoning that an established club moving into the area would prove beneficial to his takings.

Although Charringtons were intending to use the land for a new housing estate, Charles Roberts was able to negotiate a deal with them inside 24 hours, guaranteeing attendances of 1,000 for home first team games and 500 for reserve fixtures and on a 21-year lease. Charles Roberts and his negotiating partner Bobby Buckle emerged from the meeting with something of a problem, for they now had two grounds and little or no funds to develop either and still had five years to run on the lease on their Northumberland Park ground.

Fortunately for Spurs, their landlord at Northumberland Park approached the club offering them a handsome sum if they would give up their lease early – Roberts and Buckle virtually bit his hand off! The sum raised was going to prove vital in turning an old nursery site known as Beckwith's Nursery into a modern football ground.

Edmonton Cricket Club groundsman John Over supervised the development of the new ground, with some of the stands at Northumberland Park being dismantled and carried over to the new

BELOW A workman demolishes the houses in Paxton Road, to make room for a new double-decker stand at White Hart Lane, 1936

site. By June 1899 the ground looked just about complete and hosted a number of events before an official opening scheduled for 4th September 1899, including a horse jumping competition and players races and a number of trial matches. Notts County provided the opposition at the official opening, and although the match was played on a Monday, 5,000 attended and paid £115 for the privilege.

For many years the ground did not have an official name. The club invited supporters to suggest a name through the local newspaper, but the response was not great and naming the ground was put off. Eventually a number of suggestions came forward – Rowel Park (a Rowel being part of a spur), Percy Park (to maintain the Hotspur link) and Gilpin Park, but eventually the ground became known as the High Road Ground prior to the First World War. Thereafter it became White Hart Lane, initially because of the White Hart public house and the fact that the main entrance to the ground was down a lane by the side of the pub. White Hart Lane itself is some three hundred or so yards away from the ground, and until that lane got renamed the Bill Nicholson

Way a few years ago, the actual address was 748 High Road!

The ground could accommodate 30,000 when originally built and steadily grew over the ensuing decades. By far the grandest building programme the club undertook was the East Stand, designed by Archibald Leitch and opened in 1934 after costing a then massive £60,000. That took the capacity of the ground up to 78,000, of which 60,000 were said to be under cover. Floodlights were first installed in 1953 and updated four years later and in 1962 the back of the Park Lane stand was converted to incorporate additional seating, available on a first come first served basis. The following year the Paxton Road stand was similarly converted.

The old West Stand was torn down in 1980 and reopened as a two tier seating stand with executive boxes in 1982. The East Stand underwent refurbishment in 1989 which drastically reduced the standing capacity at The Shelf, but events at Hillsborough later the same year would eventually mean that White

Hart Lane, like all major stadia, had to become all-seated. The Park Lane stand was rebuilt in 1995, incorporating a giant Jumbotron screen in the roof structure, and a similar stand was built at the Paxton Road end in 1998. As there is no scope for extending the ground as it currently stands, consideration has apparently been given to demolishing the West Stand and building a bigger three tier stand in its place. The current capacity is 36,237 and the ground is effectively full for every home match.

ABOVE Aerial view of White Hart Lane, 1951

Woodgate

SPURS' LATE JANUARY SWOOP FOR the transfer of Jonathan Woodgate surprised many, not least Spurs own fans, but the continued injury problems facing Ledley King made the acquisition of a experience central defender something of a priority. Jonathan, born in Middlesbrough on 22 January 1980, is not without his own injury problems, with various ailments having blighted his career at Leeds United, Newcastle United, Real Madrid (he sat out the whole of his first year in the Spanish capital) and Middlesbrough, but on his day he is as good as any of his rivals, as evidenced by the six caps he has collected for England during his career. Less than a month after arriving at White Hart Lane he added to his trophy cabinet, netting the all important winner in the Carling Cup Final against Chelsea at Wembley with a header in extra time. During the course of the game he showed exactly what kind of partnership he could form with Ledley King as the pair kept the likes of Didier Drogba and Nicholas Anelka quiet for virtually the whole of the 120 minutes. Whilst Spurs fans will be hoping that Ledley can overcome his troublesome injuries, many will be spending just as much time praying that Jonathan Woodgate has turned the fitness corner.

Xmas Day

UP UNTIL 1958 THERE WAS A FULL League programme on Christmas Day (unless it fell on a Sunday) and often the two sides would then meet in the return fixture the following day, Boxing Day! Since most teams travelled on scheduled trains to away fixtures, this often meant that the two sides would accompany each other down from one match to the next!

1908	Oldham Athletic	A	0-1
1909	Nottingham Forest	H	2-2
1911	Woolwich Arsenal	H	5-0
1912	Manchester City	A	2-2
1914	Sheffield Wednesday	A	2-3
1919	Hull City	H	4-0
1920	Newcastle United	A	1-1
1922	Sheffield United	H	2-1
1923	Huddersfield Town	H	1-0
1924	Bury	H	1-1
1925	Birmingham City	A	1-3
1926	Manchester United	H	1-1

1928	Reading	H	2-2
1929	Southampton	H	3-2
1930	Southampton	H	1-3
1931	Charlton Athletic	H	0-1
1933	Huddersfield Town	H	1-3
1934	Grimsby Town	A	0-3
1935	Plymouth Argyle	H	1-2
1936	Blackburn Rovers	A	4-0
1937	Bury	A	2-1
1946	Coventry City	A	1-3
1947	Chesterfield	H	3-0
1948	Leicester City	A	2-1
1950	Derby County	A	1-1
1951	Charlton Athletic	A	3-0
1952	Middlesbrough	H	7-2
1953	Portsmouth	H	1-1
1954	Bolton Wanderers	A	2-1
1956	Everton	H	6-0
1958	West Ham United	A	1-2

Youth Team

SPURS HAVE won the FA Youth Cup on three occasions, 1970, 1974 and 1990. The first victory, over Coventry City, was a drawn out affair that required a replay before Spurs, featuring future first team player Barry Daines and a then unknown Scottish youngster called Graeme Souness, finally won 4-3 on aggregate.

Four years later Huddersfield were beaten 2-1 on aggregate and the side featured Chris Jones, Noel Brotherston and another relatively unknown Scottish youngster called Neil McNab.

Spurs' most recent victory came in 1990 with a 3-2 win over Middlesbrough and future first teamers who starred included Ian Walker, Ian Hendon, David Tuttle, Scott Houghton and Stuart Nethercott.

Twice Spurs have finished on the losing side in the final, beaten 2-1 on aggregate by West Ham in 1981 and 6-5 on penalties by Manchester United in 1995.

Zokora

LEFT Didier Zokora runs with the ball during a match at White Hart Lane, May 2007

BELOW Didier Zokora in action

SPURS PULLED OFF TWO TRANSFER coups during the summer of 2006, signing Dmitar Berbatov from Bayer Leverkusen and adding Didier Zokora from St Etienne a month later. Just like Berbatov, Didier had been linked with a number of English clubs prior to signing for Spurs, including Arsenal, Chelsea and Manchester United and even Real Madrid of Spain. His £8.6 million switch to White Hart Lane took many by surprise, especially as two of his best friends in football, Kolo Toure and Emmanuel Eboue had joined Arsenal; Didier signing for Spurs made him an instant crowd favourite!

Born in Abidjan on 14th December 1980 Didier is a graduate of the ASEC Abidjan academy in the Ivory Coast and made his name when he joined Genk of Belgium in 2000. A total of 126 appearances over the next four months marked him out as a defensive midfielder of some considerable note, prompting a move to St Etienne in the summer of 2004. The higher profile of the French League soon sparked a race among the bigger clubs of Europe, a race duly won by Spurs, aided in part by the fact that Spurs' director of football Damien Comoli had previously been responsible for Didier's move to St Etienne! Comoli did an impressive job in selling Spurs to Didier; Didier has done an impressive job in Spurs' midfield since he arrived. He has also won 41 caps for the Ivory Coast.

The pictures in this book were provided courtesy of the following:

GETTY IMAGES
101 Bayham Street, London NW1 0AG

PA PHOTOS
paphotos.com

Creative Director Kevin Gardner

Published by Green Umbrella Publishing

Publishers Jules Gammond & Vanessa Gardner

Written by Graham Betts